Cambridge Elements

Elements in Applied Linguistics
edited by
Li Wei
University College London
Zhu Hua
University College London

AVIATION ENGLISH AS A GLOBAL LINGUA FRANCA

Hyejeong Kim
The Hong Kong Polytechnic University

Shaftesbury Road, Cambridge CB2 8EA, United Kingdom

One Liberty Plaza, 20th Floor, New York, NY 10006, USA

477 Williamstown Road, Port Melbourne, VIC 3207, Australia

314–321, 3rd Floor, Plot 3, Splendor Forum, Jasola District Centre,
New Delhi – 110025, India

Cambridge University Press is part of Cambridge University Press & Assessment,
a department of the University of Cambridge.

We share the University's mission to contribute to society through the pursuit of
education, learning and research at the highest international levels of excellence.

www.cambridge.org
Information on this title: www.cambridge.org/9781009660754

DOI: 10.1017/9781009660785

© Hyejeong Kim 2026

This publication is in copyright. Subject to statutory exception and to the provisions
of relevant collective licensing agreements, no reproduction of any part may take
place without the written permission of Cambridge University Press & Assessment.

When citing this work, please include a reference to the DOI 10.1017/9781009660785

First published 2026

A catalogue record for this publication is available from the British Library

*A Cataloging-in-Publication data record for this Element is available from the Library
of Congress*

ISBN 978-1-009-66075-4 Hardback
ISBN 978-1-009-66080-8 Paperback
ISSN 2633-5069 (online)
ISSN 2633-5050 (print)

Cambridge University Press & Assessment has no responsibility for the persistence
or accuracy of URLs for external or third-party internet websites referred to in this
publication and does not guarantee that any content on such websites is, or will remain,
accurate or appropriate.

For EU product safety concerns, contact us at Calle de José Abascal, 56, 1°, 28003
Madrid, Spain, or email eugpsr@cambridge.org

Aviation English as a Global Lingua Franca

Elements in Applied Linguistics

DOI: 10.1017/9781009660785
First published online: February 2026

Hyejeong Kim
The Hong Kong Polytechnic University
Author for correspondence: Hyejeong Kim, hyejeong.kim@polyu.edu.hk

Abstract: This Element examines aviation English as a global lingua franca through the lens of communities of practice. Pilots and air traffic controllers involved in international operations belong to multiple communities, including local professional, broader local aviation, and international aviation communities. Their ongoing learning within these communities and the repertoire they develop – which influences their interactions – are explored. Against this framework, the inadequacy of the current internationally applicable language proficiency requirements is critically evaluated, alongside an analysis of four notable aircraft accidents that motivated these standards. The focus then shifts to analysing live radiotelephony discourse in abnormal situations, incorporating insights from domain specialists. Findings show that language-related aspects alone are insufficient; when combined with limited domain knowledge, it can lead to unsafe and ineffective communication. The Element highlights accommodation – both for linguistic and domain-specific – as a crucial skill in this intercultural communication context and recommends greater standardisation for handling abnormal situations.

Keywords: English as a lingua franca, aviation English, pilot–air traffic controller communication, communities of practice, communication accommodation theory

© Hyejeong Kim 2026

ISBNs: 9781009660754 (HB), 9781009660808 (PB), 9781009660785 (OC)
ISSNs: 2633-5069 (online), 2633-5050 (print)

Contents

1 Introduction   1

2 Aviation English as a Global Lingua Franca within Communities of Practice   4

3 International Civil Aviation Organisation and English Proficiency Requirements   26

4 Discourse Analysis and Domain Specialists' Evaluations   39

5 Discussion and Recommendations   60

References   73

1 Introduction

The English language has long served as the global lingua franca in aviation, officially since 1944 (ICAO, 1944), and it remains the most widely used lingua franca in this industry today. Historically, the choice appeared obvious given the influence of the United States (US) in aviation, including the presence of English-speaking ex-military pilots and major aircraft manufacturers (Crystal, 2003). Had the decision been made today, the outcome would likely be the same; English's dominance continues to grow with no competing language in the foreseeable future. English is also widely used as a lingua franca in many other professional sectors, such as business and healthcare, due to increasing global mobility. Consequently, there has been a growing body of research on English as a lingua franca (ELF), particularly in fields such as academia and business.

Public attention to communication between pilots and air traffic controllers (hereafter 'controllers') has been sporadic, primarily arising when communication issues are reported in the media as contributing factors to accidents and incidents. Academic attention from applied linguistics started growing after the International Civil Aviation Organisation (ICAO), a United Nations specialised agency, adopted English proficiency requirements in 2003 in response to concerns that insufficient English proficiency among 'non-native' English-speaking pilots and controllers had contributed to past accidents. While specialised coded radiotelephony language is used in routine situations, more natural English is expected in abnormal or emergency situations, where communication shifts to English as a lingua franca. In these contexts, ICAO maintains that English proficiency is crucial. Accordingly, all 'non-native' English-speaking pilots and controllers are required to demonstrate proficiency by taking a test assessing six criteria: *pronunciation*, *comprehension*, *structure*, *vocabulary*, *fluency*, and *interactions*. Proficiency is evaluated on a scale from pre-elementary level 1 to expert level 6, with level 4 set as the minimum operational requirement. So-called 'native speakers' are effectively exempt, as their inherent proficiency is assumed to be at expert level 6 unless a speech impediment or excessively strong regional accent is detected during licensure (ICAO, 2022, n.d.). However, the criteria for evaluating these qualities – especially, who judges and on what basis internationally inappropriate accents are assessed – remain unclear, as does the assumption of expert competence in radiotelephony communication by being 'native speakers'. This effectively imposes a 'non-native speaker' identity on pilots and controllers who use English as an additional language (L2+), framing them as deficient in competence (Holliday, 2018; Piller & Bodis, 2022) and thus affecting their performance (discussed in Sections 4 and 5).

There is also a recurring policy regarding proficiency verification. Pilots and controllers who meet the minimum level 4 must retake a test every three years, while those at level 5 are tested every six years. This limited shelf life is somewhat questionable, given that pilots and controllers continuously learn through ongoing practice. Here 'learning' should not be understood in the second language acquisition sense but rather as engagement and development within communities of practice, which include members whose first language (L1) is English and L2+ members (discussed in detail in Section 2).

ICAO's English proficiency requirements aimed for effectiveness by 2008, with a three-year transition period extending the deadline to March 2011. However, two months before this deadline, 137 of 191 (close to 72 per cent) member states at that time had not yet complied. Service providers in Italy and Romania claimed that all aviation personnel met the minimum level (Alderson, 2011). According to a report from Korea (Aviation Policy Division, 2009), many L2+ member states – including China, France, Indonesia, Japan, Korea, Russia, and Taiwan – developed their own tests at the government level or national airline level. Alderson's surveys (2009, 2010, 2011), however, raised doubts about the quality of these tests, revealing that many testing organisations failed to provide sufficient, or indeed any, evidence of test quality and that their assessment processes fell short of international language testing standards. Fifteen years after policy implementation, only one test (the English Language Proficiency for Aeronautical Communication) has received ICAO's recommendation. ICAO operates by member state consent and lacks authority to mandate policies, respecting member states' sovereignty (MacKenzie, 2010). Thus, while all member states agreed to the policy, which had been proposed in the name of safety – since not agreeing could be viewed as a loss of face – some or many L2+ states developed and implemented tests to maintain control and minimise the policy's impact. In this context, questions arise regarding the rationale behind such responses by member states when their own safety is at stake, and whether the policy overlooks critical aspects of the target language use situation.

Performance and communication in professional settings are shaped by numerous interconnected elements, including work culture, values, history, relationships, domain knowledge, experience, expertise, and both language- and domain-specific aspects (e.g., Kim, 2018; Kim & Elder, 2009; Kim & Friginal, 2026). These elements can best be examined within the framework of *communities of practice*. In broader investigations of ELF, which predominantly occurs in intercultural contexts where English is used for specific purposes, the suitability of this framework – as opposed to the concept of a *speech community* – has been acknowledged but not thoroughly explored. Accordingly, this study aims to investigate the various aspects influencing aviation ELF, with a particular focus on pilot and controller performance and radiotelephony communication, and to situate these within the community of practice framework. Additionally, it reviews ICAO English proficiency requirements from this perspective. To address these aims, the study responds to the following research questions:

1. What language-specific and domain-specific aspects emerge from domain specialists' evaluations of peers' performance in naturally occurring situations?
2. How do domain specialists' values inform the understanding of performance in radiotelephony within the framework of communities of practice?
3. What are the implications of domain specialists' values for ICAO's English proficiency requirements?

In the following section, Section 2, I attempt to identify multiple aviation communities of practice within the international community by drawing on key concepts from the framework, such as legitimate periphery participation, learning through practice and interaction among members, and evolving identities leading to expertise. To gain a deeper understanding of the international context, I contextualise radiotelephony communication by explaining the environmental challenges posed by voice-only communication. I then highlight shared and unshared repertoires among members of the international community. Shared repertoires relate to rules-based conventions developed in response to the environment challenges inherent in radiotelephony communication, while unshared repertoires pertain to the individual variations that members bring to this international context, constituting significant challenges for radiotelephony communication. To address these variations, accommodation skills, explored in pilot-controller interaction as well as in ELF studies in other contexts, are suggested as a way forward. Building on this background, Section 3 details the ICAO English proficiency requirements and critiques found in the literature, followed by an examination of differing interpretations and perceptions related to four frequently cited aircraft accidents that ICAO used to justify the establishment of the English proficiency standards. Moving from these extreme cases to more commonly occurring abnormal cases, Section 4 presents an instance of naturally occurring performance, drawing on domain specialists' insights as they evaluate the performance captured in the recording. In Section 5, I discuss the findings reported in Section 4 in relation to the three research questions: the values that emerge as domain specialists evaluate their peers' performance, how these values can be understood within the framework of communities of practice, and implications for ICAO's English proficiency requirements. The Element then concludes with brief remarks.

2 Aviation English as a Global Lingua Franca within Communities of Practice

Originating from a social theory of learning, the concept of communities of practice is a well-established, practice-based model developed by social anthropologist Jean Lave and educational theorist and practitioner Etienne Wenger (Lave, 2019; Lave & Wenger, 1991; Wenger, 1998). The suitability of this concept for describing ELF communication contexts has been recognised by scholars in the field (e.g., Canagarajah, 2007; Ehrenreich, 2017; House, 2003; Seidlhofer, 2009), particularly in contrast to the concept of the *speech community*, which focusses on shared norms or a single linguistic variety in a community (Hymes, 1972; Labov, 1972), such as Australian English and British English. ELF communication, which often occurs beyond the boundaries of traditional speech communities, takes place in intercultural contexts where interactants from diverse linguistic and cultural backgrounds engage with one another. House (2003) briefly mentions the potential suitability of the communities of practice framework for capturing the interactional features of ELF, while Canagarajah (2007) argues that the practice-based nature of this model makes it particularly well-suited for understanding ELF realisations. Indeed, there are no shared norms or single varieties that can fully explain ELF interactions. On the contrary, as Canagarajah (2007) contends, the variation that each individual brings to the interaction and the ways in which participants manage these variations, are central to these communicative exchanges. The focus of ELF research is on communicative features that emerge in interactions; however, to fully understand the complexity of these contexts, it is necessary to adopt a broader approach. Accordingly, this section attempts to do so by situating aviation communities within the communities of practice framework.

The concept of apprenticeship is important in examining communities of practice. In Lave and Wenger's (1991) earlier book, descriptions are provided of apprenticeships in five different communities of practice: Yucatec midwives, tailors, naval quartermasters, meat cutters, and nondrinking alcoholics, as well as a medical claims processing centre discussed in Wenger's (1998) later book. The contexts of Yucatec midwives, tailors, and meat cutters evoke a somewhat archaic sense of outdated times, seemingly irrelevant to the present day. However, by citing a mathematical problem-solving activity undertaken by a member of a family – where the family is considered a community of practice in this case – during everyday grocery shopping in a supermarket (Murtaugh, 1985), Lave (2019) convincingly demonstrates what occurs in everyday mathematical practice, which differs significantly from conventional conceptions of math problem solving. In Murtaugh (1985):

> I just keep putting them in until I think there's enough. There's only about three or four [apples] at home, and I have four kids, so you figure at least two apiece in the next three days. These are the kinds of things I have to resupply. I only have a certain amount of storage space in the refrigerator, so I can't load it up totally ... Now that I'm home in the summertime, this is a good snack food. And I like an apple sometimes at lunchtime when I come home. (p. 188)

Lave (2019) explains that although apprenticeships are ubiquitous, they are often not recognised as learning in practice or apprenticeships because they are considered informal and thus are less valued or overlooked in most modern education systems. She further argues that apprenticeship studies, in the anthropological sense, provide a means to explore how learning occurs independently of formal teaching. She notes that apprenticeship differs from schooling or socialisation in that it is always situated within practice. Lave (2019) also observes that we are all apprentices within the communities of practice to which we belong, such as the shopper in Murtaugh's study mentioned earlier, with home or family serving as a community of practice.

Lave (2019) conceptualises learning as engagement with others within communities of practice – in other words, learning through practice – and identifies 'changes in knowledge and action' as central to the process of apprenticeship. Thus, Lave and Wenger (1991) and Lave (2019) argue that communities of practice themselves provide learning opportunities for all members, whether peripheral (i.e., newer) or old-timers (i.e., more experienced), as they participate within them. In this framework, learning is always understood as situated in everyday (work) life, occurring sometimes through observation of more experienced individuals or peers with lower levels of participation, and at other times through medium-level, active, or fuller participation while engaged in practice. Additionally, as newer members move from their peripheral participation to fuller participation, and as senior members leave communities of practice, they contribute historical traces of artefacts, including physical, linguistic, and symbolic forms, along with social structures. In this way, practices are constituted and reconstituted over time (Lave & Wenger, 1991).

Building on this background, I situate aviation communication within the framework of communities of practice. This will help understand radiotelephony communication between pilots and controllers, who bring their values, perceptions, and work cultures, among others, from both local and international communities into their interactions. First, I discuss the unique multiple memberships held by pilots and controllers engaged in international radio communication. Next, I explore the concept of learning in practice and the evolving identities within the international aviation community of practice. I then examine the elements that constitute this international community, including environmental challenges and both shared and unshared repertoires among its members. Lastly, I review accommodation as a strategy to bridge gaps in unshared repertoires, drawing on insights from ELF research in other contexts.

2.1 Multiple Memberships

In the context of international aviation, pilots and controllers hold multiple memberships across several different but interrelated communities of practice, as summarised in Figure 1. The following description is based on a one-day nonparticipant observation of three air traffic control units in Korea, supplemented by audio-recorded explanations provided by controllers in each unit, as well as my long-standing interactions with pilots and controllers and my research on aviation communication.

There are three main communities of practice: those of pilots, controllers, and the combined community of pilots and controllers. Additionally, within and across these communities, individual memberships may vary depending on position and level of expertise. With increasing mobility in recent years, airline companies themselves have become multicultural contexts. For example, approximately half of the captain pilots in one Korean airline are foreign nationals (Kim, forthcoming), and the situation is likely similar in other airlines globally. In contrast, all controllers in Korea are Korean civil servants due to security reasons, although some countries do hire foreign citizens as controllers.

Pilots are considered first. Their multiple community memberships depend on their position, profession, and nationality. For instance, a Korean pilot might belong to the community of first officers or captains, while simultaneously holding membership as a pilot at the company level, the national level, and as a Korean pilot within the international aviation community. Within and across these communities, pilots closely interact to practise their profession, whether working with long-term partners or complete strangers in the cockpit. They collaborate as first officers and captains, sharing information and experience among all members. For instance, when unusual or unique features arise regarding certain air routes, airports, or language habits of specific L1 groups, pilots may share relevant information and personal experiences. During flights, first officers and captains collaborate closely, though the captain bears greater responsibility and is relied upon more heavily for expertise and experience.

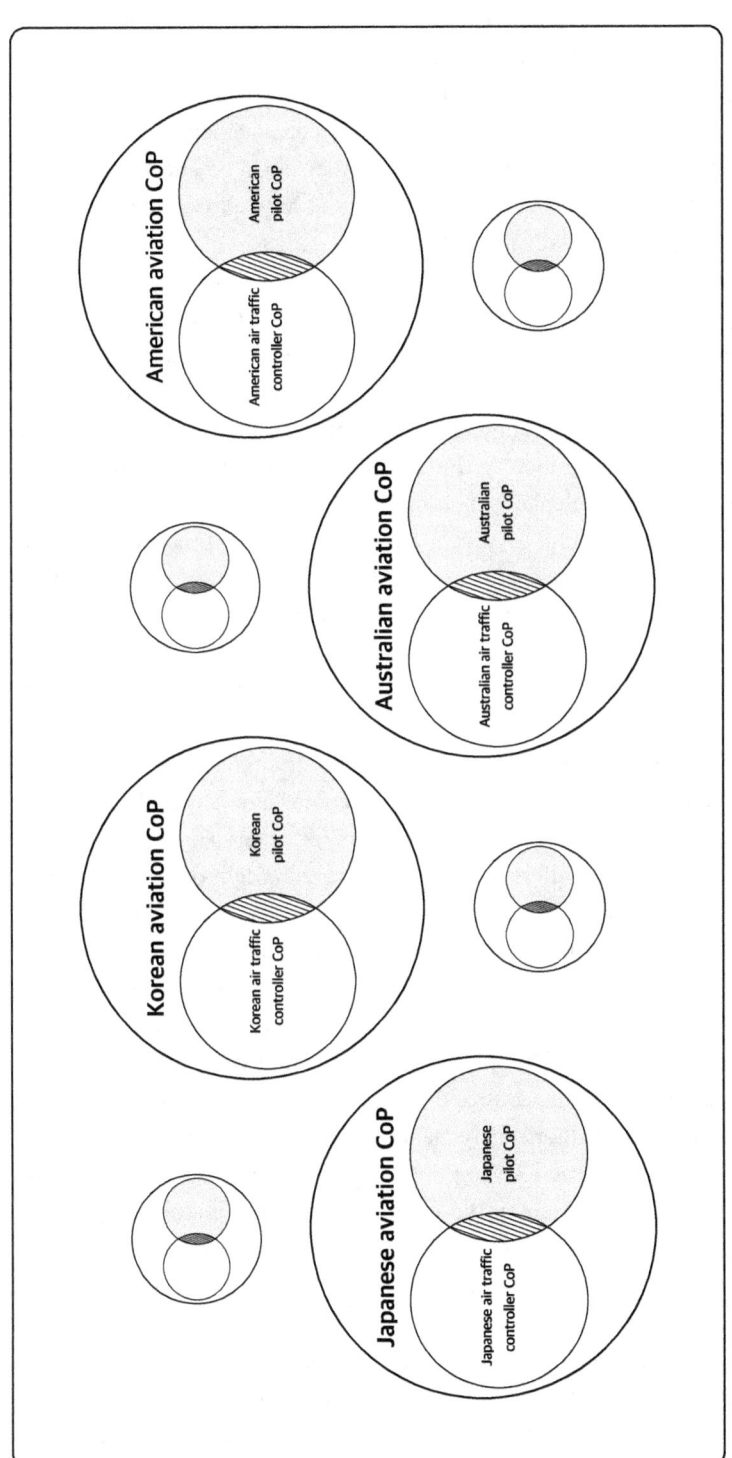

Figure 1 International aviation community of practice (CoP)

Roles and rules are expected, and as pilots advance in their careers within particular teams, these roles and rules become increasingly routinised and tacitly understood rather than explicitly defined (e.g., Hutchins & Klausen, 1996). Within these multiple communities, mutual engagement varies in intensity. Among colleagues who operate flights together, engagement is grounded in everyday practice; however, this smaller community may change as their positions and experience evolve over time.

Controllers, like pilots, also have multiple and overlapping community memberships. However, their communities typically maintain more stable relationships at the local level, with members familiar with each other's career trajectories. Controllers belong to the team with which they work most closely, the associated air traffic control unit (ground, approach, or en route control), and the broader controller community. Extensive coordination is required as air traffic control and radiotelephony communication are handed over from one unit to another. Controllers working in en route units in Korea, for example, actively interact with counterparts in neighbouring countries such as China, Japan, and North Korea for coordination purposes. Furthermore, smaller, hierarchically arranged communities of practice exist within each unit, including trainee controllers working under supervision until they obtain full certification, colleagues working within or across teams, team leaders, and supervisors overseeing entire units. Given this hierarchical structure, when unusual or unexpected situations arise, less experienced controllers can seek assistance from more experienced colleagues, team leaders, or supervisors.

As both pilots and controllers collaborate closely in flight operations and air traffic control – a dynamic not depicted in Figure 1 – they form a distinct community of practice, characterised by intensive, though non-face-to-face, radiotelephony communication. The practices of each group are closely interwoven. Pilots operate flights based on instructions or information received from controllers throughout all flight phases, communicating with multiple controllers from departure to arrival. Controllers, meanwhile, manage air traffic within their units and may simultaneously handle numerous aircraft from various countries. They issue instructions to pilots and sometimes request information to ensure safe and efficient air traffic control. Since their interaction is never face-to-face, it presents a significant challenge because one aspect of communication, nonverbal communication, is unavailable. Nonverbal communication can sometimes repeat, conflict with, complement, substitute, accentuate, or regulate verbal communication; thus, its absence can affect the completeness and effectiveness of communication (Knapp et al., 2014). Consequently, strict adherence to radiotelephony procedures and conventions is essential for safety and efficiency. This form of communication relies on standard phraseology in routine situations, a specialised language developed for radiotelephony, which includes acronyms and technical jargon (see Section 2.3.2 for further details).

The system of radiotelephony communication practised by the pilot and controller is highly rigorous, involving well-defined and strictly regulated duties, roles, and language use (e.g., Varantola, 1989). Violations of these duties and roles result in sanctions, such as letters issued to the associated airline or government agency detailing the nature of the violation. When flight operations or air traffic control procedures deviate from routine – that is, during unexpected or abnormal situations – departures from established protocols become more likely. Nevertheless, even in these abnormal circumstances, expected duties and roles associated with the broader community of practice remain, allowing members to judge the appropriateness of behaviour in context.

Differences do exist across the various communities to which pilots and controllers belong. While the core dimensions of practice are shared across the entire international community at the broadest level, particular values and norms may be shared and appreciated only within certain narrower communities. For this reason, the traits of specific national aviation communities of practice – including work culture, character, and language use habits – are often noted by members of the international community. Moreover, there is not always consensus on how such characteristics are evaluated. Certain practices within the American aviation community of practice are often criticised for their habitual violation of radiotelephony conventions (e.g., Hawkins & Orlady, 2017; Kim & Friginal, 2026), due to differing and potentially conflicting conceptions and levels of awareness among its members. These differences stem from individual experience, expertise, L1s, attitudes, and the organisational cultures of the smaller communities to which pilots and controllers belong.

2.2 Learning in Practice and Changing Identities

Learning through practice and evolving identities along trajectories are core concepts within the community of practice framework (Lave, 2019; Lave & Wenger, 1991). As newcomers join a community of practice, their learning begins through *legitimate peripheral participation*. Legitimacy signifies their belonging to the community; as members, they engage in and perform their roles while assuming their share of responsibility. Lave and Wenger (1991) stress that the concept of the periphery should be understood from the structural perspective of communities of practice. With experienced members or old-timers (e.g., captains) participating more fully, peripheral members learn and advance towards greater participations, and in doing so, their identities also change – for example, from individuals who learn a particular skill through practice to individuals who have experience in that skill. In the longer term, their participation within the community of practice increases. To illustrate this within the pilot community of practice, the description by one pilot informant who participated in the study by Kim and Friginal (2026) of his first communication with Mumbai and Colombo controllers as a first officer, and how he learned from a senior captain in the cockpit, is revealing – in this case, in a quite explicit way:

> We have to talk to Mumbai and Colombo a lot . . . If you don't know what to expect, when they talk to you, trying to ascertain what they are asking for is really difficult . . . my first flight across, I hadn't done that particular procedure on the HF [High Frequency] before. I was flying with the captain; I was on the radio . . . Mumbai contacted us and the accent was so thick . . . I looked straight at the captain. I was like, 'oh . . . I'm sorry I didn't. Did you? Did you catch any of that?' And because he had heard it before a hundred times, and he knew exactly what they're asking for. I think that knowing what to expect in that situation really facilitated his understanding of what they were trying to achieve on the radio. So he was like, 'just watch me do the first one, and then you can do so.' He did. He talked to Colombo and Sri Lanka on the radio, and then said, 'yeah, this is the format you do use for the HF position report' and then and after that, talking to Mumbai, it was so much easier to understand what they were asking. And even though the accent was quite thick.

This pilot informant described the encountered situation – a procedural report communicated via high-frequency radio – that was complicated by unfamiliar accents. Learning occurred through practice while participating alongside a more experienced senior member in the cockpit. With his accumulated knowledge and skills from performing similar tasks, his understanding developed relatively quickly. As illustrated by this example, pilots gain experience through everyday practice, and their identities evolve into those of individuals capable of managing such situations; this process is understood as learning (Lave, 2019).

When learning is understood this way, it becomes clearer that the communities of practice framework originates from a social theory of learning. Lave (2019) argues that learning is a social process that occurs through interaction, rather than an individual process taking place solely within the mind of the learner, as is traditionally and more commonly understood in psychology. The author further explains that situatedness, or context, is crucial for learning, and experiencing it within its situated context is what defines apprenticeship. In the context of the anecdotes illustrated over Mumbai and Colombo earlier, the pilot informant's learning is not something that could be acquired in advance, such as during a pre-flight briefing. It becomes meaningful only within the situated context, given the complexity of the challenges compounded by the peculiarity of that specific airspace and the unfamiliar accents. Citing Coy's introductory chapter on the theory of apprenticeship, which describes apprenticeship training as 'personal, hands-on, and experiential' (Coy, 1989, p. 1), Lave (2019) emphasises the practice aspect, noting that apprentices, or legitimate peripheral participants, are becoming skilled practitioners within specialised occupations. This process of apprenticeship involves more than socialisation – for example, all children are socialised within a given society – but entails learning specialised skills and knowledge through practice. A practice is 'a way of doing things, as grounded in and shared by a community' (Eckert & Wenger, 2005, p. 583), and through apprenticeship, not only knowledge and skills but also 'appropriate deportment, shared assumptions, behaviours and values (i.e., culture)' (Cooper, 1989, p. 137) are transmitted.

The cultures of the communities of practice to which pilots and controllers belong are situated at both local and international levels, with the local level influencing the international level. Although differences and conflicts can arise within local communities, they are generally more manageable compared to those found in the international community. When unshared cultural elements present challenges, bridging these differences may be more difficult due to the greater diversity and potential conflicts among the many aggregated communities within the global context. Nevertheless, the international aviation community of practice as a whole shares a clear common goal: safe and efficient flight operations.

2.3 International Aviation Community of Practice

This section provides a closer examination of the international aviation community of practice. Pilots and controllers interact in a unique manner – exclusively through radiotelephony. While they engage in face-to-face practice within their local communities, such as in the cockpit and the associated air traffic control unit, they simultaneously communicate over radio, which constitutes the international context of their community. ICAO specifies rules and procedures for radiotelephony communication; thus, these are intended to form a shared culture, a way of doing things. However, differing values, interpretations, language backgrounds, and work cultures challenge this ideal, resulting in gaps and conflicts. These issues are explained in turn.

2.3.1 Environmental Challenges

As briefly mentioned in Section 2.1, the non-face-to-face communication environment itself poses many challenges due to the absence of aiding non-verbal cues. Moreover, aircraft noise and equipment-related sounds add an additional layer of complexity to this environment, making clear communication even more challenging. As noise levels increase, intelligibility decreases, particularly when communication relies solely on auditory cues rather than on both auditory and visual cues, as is the case in radiotelephony (Hawkins & Orlady, 2017). Since English is a global lingua franca, do aviation communities with English L1 pilots and controllers have an advantage in radio communication and are they less vulnerable to challenges in this environment? Studies show that it is not the case. While the benefit of a shared L1 has yielded mixed results in studies (e.g., Bent & Bradlow, 2003; Major et al., 2002), Adank et al. (2009) demonstrated that familiarity with a particular accent plays a significant role under noisy conditions. Their participants from Glasgow, who were familiar with both Received Pronunciation (e.g., through media) and Glaswegian accents, showed comparable comprehension in both normal and noise conditions. In contrast, participants from Greater London, who were familiar only with Received Pronunciation, exhibited slower responses in noise conditions. Some studies have focussed on the distinction between 'native' and 'non-native' speakers in terms of intelligibility and perception (e.g., Molesworth et al., 2014; Shimizu et al., 2002; van Wijngaarden et al., 2002), showing that noise conditions tend to affect L2+ users more adversely.

In pilot-controller interaction, Tiewtrakul and Fletcher's (2010) study on accent effects, based on radiotelephony discourse from Bangkok international airport, where controllers are all Thai L1 speakers, found a shared L1 advantage: communication between Thai pilots and controllers involved fewer errors, followed by interaction with English L1 pilots, and then non-Thai L2+ pilots. While emphasising the critical impact of accents, the authors recommend more rigorous training for L2+ pilots and controllers. However, this distinction between 'native' and 'non-native', commonly found in second language acquisition studies – which often focus on how 'non-native' English use differs from that of so-called 'natives' – can also be interpreted in terms of familiarity and unfamiliarity. In ELF contexts, this distinction is largely irrelevant and unhelpful, as shared understanding and mutual responsibility for the success or failure of communication are paramount, regardless of speakers' L1s or 'native' status (Kim & Billington, 2018; Kim & Elder, 2009). Instead, the ability to manage a variety of accents – whether this is more challenging or easier – can serve as a valuable measure of communicative competence in these contexts. Research on the benefit of familiarity with different accents, particularly through long-term exposure, is illuminating in this regard, as evidenced by studies conducted in settings such as Hong Kong (Tauroza & Luk, 1997) and the US (Smith & Nelson, 2020). Smith and Nelson's study shows that intelligibility (recognising words and utterances) was easier for the participants than comprehensibility (understanding meaning) and interpretability (inferring intended meaning). Although the English L1 group performed better in comprehensibility, the group more familiar with diverse English accents was better at accurately interpreting interactions. The authors highlight that increasing varieties of English do not hinder understanding, provided users develop familiarity with them.

2.3.2 Shared Repertoire among Members

To address environmental challenges in radiotelephony communication and the complexity of interactions between pilots and controllers, *standard phraseology* was developed. ICAO's (1996) nine basic principles of phraseology can be summarised as follows: (1) English should serve as the basis; (2) selected words and phrases must ensure optimum transmissibility without risk of misinterpretation; (3) words and phrases prone to pronunciation variations should be avoided; (4) commonly used spoken Q codes, such as QFE and QNH[1], may be preferred over lengthy or complex phrases; (5) phrases proven phonetically effective across languages should remain unchanged; (6) new phrases should be clear, unambiguous, and concise without sacrificing clarity for brevity; (7) phrases should convey a thought in natural language using the simplest grammar; (8) positive and negative instructions should be clearly distinguished; (9) where possible, avoid words with sounds or syllables difficult for 'non-native' English speakers to pronounce. In short, clarity, resistance to misinterpretation, and maximum transmissibility are of paramount importance. Currently, the ICAO standard phraseology (ICAO, 2007) comprises 553 phrases, with 231 allocated for tower control (e.g., *report when ready for departure*) – including 28 for airport ground vehicle or crew service –, 209 for approach control (e.g., *FL80 estimating north cross 46 information delta*), and 113 for en route control (e.g., *stop descent at FL150*) (Kim & Zhang, forthcoming). In the literature, standard phraseology is described as the most successful semi-artificial international language (Robertson, 1987), a purpose-built language (Varantola, 1989), or a codified language (Philps, 1991). Robertson highlights the difficulty that English L1 pilots and controllers face in strictly adhering to standard phraseology, as natural English is often easier and more convenient to use. He notes:

> Standard behaviour does not come naturally—even on the purely procedural, as opposed to the linguistic, side, complaints about sloppy RT [radiotelephony] discipline are commonly heard ... Natural languages are never static,

---

[1] QFE: Atmospheric pressure at aerodrome elevation (or at runway threshold) and QNH: Altimeter subscale setting to obtain elevation when on the ground (ICAO, 2010).

their users impose change continuously ... RT phraseology goes against nature and has to counter the same influences which are otherwise given free rein in natural language. (p. ix).

Similarly, Varantola (1989) notes that L2+ pilots and controllers find it easier to use standard phraseology because they learn the code and use it in context with less interference, whereas English L1 pilots and controllers must consciously distinguish between the code and the natural language they use in other contexts. For this reason, Estival (2016, 2025) argues that English L1 pilots and controllers need to learn and practise standard phraseology as if it were a second language.

The deletions and omissions (e.g., subjects, linking verbs, or prepositions) typical of phraseology sub-grammar are possible because the language is embedded within referential meanings specific to the flight phase and air traffic control context, rendering certain elements redundant (Philps, 1991). Additionally, at the surface level, even a simple list of phrases within a single transmission (e.g., four noun phrases in juxtaposition – *runway 35, wind 340 degrees 10 knots, QNH 1008, no traffic*) can be meaningful without causing confusion, as the messages are conveyed within well-defined operational and procedural contexts (Kim & Zhang, forthcoming).

To ensure clarity over radio, numbers such as those for flight levels and radio frequencies are pronounced according to specific guidelines. Notably, distinctive pronunciations include three as [triː] and thousand as [taʊzənd], due to the difficulty some users have in pronouncing the voiceless dental fricative /θ/; and five as [faɪf] and nine as [naɪnər] to avoid phonetic confusion (Philps, 1991), as the initial and final sounds in [faɪv] and [naɪn] in natural English can become indistinct in noisy conditions (Trippe & Baese-Berk, 2019). Similarly, airport names and geographical points on the map are coded using letters from the phonetic alphabet to avoid ambiguity caused by variations in pronunciation (e.g., *a* for alpha, *b* for bravo ... *y* for yankee, and *z* for zulu). The most notable conventions are *readback* and *hearback*. Messages provided by the controller must be repeated by the pilot to ensure that the instructions are correctly received; this procedure is called readback. The controller then listens to verify whether the messages read back by the pilot are correct. This procedure is known as hearback. During the hearback process, if a pilot's partial or incorrect understanding is detected, the controller is required to correct it (e.g., by using the phrase *negative, I say again* ...).

The readback and hearback monitoring practices embedded in radiotelephony communication serve as pre-emptive systems to prevent misunderstanding or lack of understanding. The hearback procedure is particularly important, as it can alter the pilot's understanding of the situation; without it, the pilot would rely solely on their own perception. This likely explains why studies in the US have focussed on nonroutine communication, where repetition of the initiate-readback process through the controller's hearback is necessary. Focussed on live radiotelephony discourse from multiple air traffic control units in the US, studies – 48 hours of tower control recordings in Burki-Cohen (1995), 42 hours of approach control in Morrow et al. (1993), and 47 hours of en route control in Cardosi (1993) – show that the readback error was remarkably low, at less than 1 per cent. While this low rate of noncompliance is reassuring in routine transmissions, it is crucial to recognise that a single piece of unclear information could have catastrophic consequences in air traffic control. Consequently, all studies emphasise the importance of pilots and controllers strictly adhering to readback and hearback procedures. Readback errors were more likely to occur when a single transmission contained multiple pieces of information (e.g., number, direction, altitude, and location) (Burki-Cohen, 1995; Cardosi, 1993) and involved two speech acts (e.g., directive and request) rather than just one (Morrow et al., 1993). With particular emphasis on compliance with standard phraseology, Howard (2008), based on an analysis of 15 hours of radiotelephony discourse, notes that deviations from standard phraseology and conventions are critical precursors to communication problems, as they inherently violate system rules and interlocutor expectations.

Drawing on the same recordings from their earlier study, Morrow et al. (1994) conducted further analysis to investigate the reasons for deviations from procedures. Two main reasons were identified: limited air traffic conventions for resolving communication problems when they arose and a lack of flexibility in these conventions for addressing nonstandard topics. The findings indicated that communication became nonroutine primarily during the acceptance of previously presented information, rather than when presenting new information. In such cases, both pilots and controllers tended to use natural English. When communication deviated from prescribed procedures, more complex syntax, nonstandard terminology, abbreviations, and context-dependent referring expressions were employed. Accordingly, the authors made three recommendations: (1) pilots and controllers should adhere to standard procedures and conventions; (2) standard procedures for nonroutine communication should be developed; and (3) training emphasising collaborative principles should be implemented. These recommendations are particularly relevant to the discourse analysis informed by insights from domain experts and will be further discussed in Section 4.

2.3.3 Unshared Repertoires among Members: Managing Variation

Variation in the individual resources that pilots and controllers bring to interactions in the international radiotelephony communication context poses challenges in this professional setting. Since pilot-controller interactions are prescribed, routinised, and proceed as expected in routine situations, such variations are unlikely to be noticeable. However, in abnormal situations, such as when an aircraft experiences a problem that does not affect its normal operation (e.g., a sick passenger on board or a diversion due to fuel shortage), or during emergencies, such variations emerge and play a significant role. For instance, a controller under close supervision may communicate with a pilot who has decades of international experience and benefit from the pilot's expertise in managing abnormal situations as they unfold through communication. An L2+ first officer flying into Sydney for the first time may appreciate accommodations made by an English L1 controller, such as a slower speech rate, in response to the pilot's perceived inexperience or unfamiliarity with the airport or accent. Conversely, a captain with substantial international experience but new to flying into New York may struggle to understand colloquial expressions used by controllers speaking rapidly during commonly occurring abnormal situations. These variations, referred to here as unshared repertoires in contrast to the shared ones discussed in the previous section, present challenges that pilots and controllers must manage to ensure effective collaboration, often emerging in complex and interconnected ways.

One notable variation is the use of *plain language* – specifically, *plain English* – referring to both the language spoken on the ground and English – when standard phraseology is unavailable, such as in abnormal or emergency situations. In these contexts, English use shifts from specialised language (i.e., standard phraseology) to English as a global lingua franca. ICAO (2010) offers somewhat contradictory explanations regarding plain language: on one hand, it states that it should be delivered in 'the same clear, concise, and unambiguous manner as standard phraseology' (p. 4–2); on the other, it describes plain language as 'the spontaneous, creative, and non-coded use of a given natural language' (p. 6–6). While the former emphasises restricted use, the latter highlights natural use. As a result, there is considerable variation in how individual pilots and controllers interpret plain English. Due to accessibility issues, however, there is a lack of studies focussing on abnormal or emergency situations. Some literature on emergency situations is available because accidents have occurred, drawing attention to these extreme cases. These cases often involve numerous factors throughout the unfolding events, which will be discussed in Section 3.

This section focusses on three intertwined variations observed in pilot-controller communication during abnormal situations, which pilots and controllers need to manage in aviation ELF contexts, as identified in my earlier studies: the use of plain English, experience and expertise, and accent familiarity. Experienced pilots and controllers served as informants in relevant studies, providing evaluations and interpretations of these scenarios. Elder et al. (2017) provide a well-argued discussion on the contributions non-language specialists can make to the constructs of communicative competence. They illustrate this through examples from two professional fields, healthcare (see Elder & McNamara, 2016; Pill, 2016) and aviation, as well as one general context (see also Sato & McNamara, 2019). Their discussion raises important questions about how narrowly language-focussed assessments, though valid from the perspective of applied linguists, may lack meaningfulness for professionals in real-world settings. A further question concerns whether such assessments are valid at all. Although exploring domain specialists' perceptions in professional contexts is not new, when these perceptions are linked to discussions of the validity of communicative constructs, the issue becomes essential rather than optional. Thus, the studies summarised in the following are particularly significant because experienced pilots and controllers, language users themselves in the international radiotelephony communication context, served as informants to evaluate naturally occurring peer performance.

Kim and Elder's (2009) study examined an abnormal situation involving a fuel shortage on a Cathay aircraft, with discourse between an American pilot and a Korean controller. Six experienced Korean aviation specialists served as informants. Due to fuel overconsumption, the American pilot initially requested a diversion to Shanghai, later changing it to Osaka while in Korean airspace. The informants noted that the pilot's transmissions were often unclear, indirect, excessively fast, and noncompliant with radiotelephony conventions, which they identified as typical of many English L1 pilots and controllers. For example, when requesting the diversion, the pilot said: *Roger sir, due to operational requirement we're having to divert and diversion port will be Shanghai. If you could er . . . liaise with Shanghai ATC and request vector for landing in Shanghai, please, Cathay 883*. The informants suggested this could have been simplified to 'request a diversion to Shanghai'. Similarly, when the Korean controller asked for the reason for diversion, the pilot said: *Cathay 883, due to strong head wind, we do not have enough fuel to reach Hong Kong, weather in Taipei is not suitable for landing. Our company would like us to go to Shanghai to refuel, Cathay 883*. The informants recommended a concise explanation such as 'due to fuel shortage'. The use of four-letter ICAO airport codes is standard to avoid confusion, especially since Shanghai has two international airports. The informants noted that the pilot should have used these codes instead of the city name. For example, Pudong airport is Zulu Sierra Papa Delta and Hongqiao airport is Zulu Sierra Sierra Sierra. This omission continued when the pilot changed the destination to Osaka (Romeo Juliett Bravo Bravo). Regarding the Korean controller, missed understanding and noncompliance with radiotelephony conventions were also observed. While attempting to clarify whether the destination was Hongqiao or Pudong, the controller failed to recognise the change to Osaka and repeatedly asked which Shanghai airport was intended. This was resolved only after the pilot specified RJBB, the ICAO code for Osaka. Additionally, the controller did not use the five-letter code, the navigational point RUGMA, which the pilot could not locate on the map, leading to extended exchanges to clarify its spelling.

The evaluations provided by the Korean domain specialist informants were consistent with those from a later replication study by Kim and Friginal (2026), which used the same audio recording but involved ten Australian domain specialist informants. The Australian informants evaluated the Korean controller more positively, emphasising his handling of the fast-speaking pilot who failed to deliver clear and direct messages, as well as the overall success of the communication. The shared values among aviation domain specialists, regardless their L1 backgrounds, concerning communication priorities and language delivery are revealing. However, the extent and degree of restriction or liberty in the use of plain English required or permitted in radiotelephony communication remain unclear due to the absence of guidelines and thus depends on individual perceptions. For instance, while the Korean informants unequivocally criticised the American pilot's verbosity, one Australian controller informant considered the American pilot's plain English use acceptable. This Australian informant also evaluated the Korean controller as lacking confidence in his use of plain English. It appears that the Korean informants, and potentially including others in L2+ communities, tend to adopt a more rigid view emphasising conciseness. In contrast, the Australian informants, and possibly others in English L1 communities, while also valuing simplicity and clarity, adopt a more flexible approach. This unresolved variation is critical in the international aviation community of practice, as individual perspectives shape local cultural norms that are transmitted to junior members, potentially perpetuating undesirable practices.

In addition to message delivery, the Korean informants deemed the American pilot's unnecessary intervention in the controller's role by instructing him to coordinate with other controllers inappropriate. Similarly, the Australian informants judged the pilot's premature contact, made before his airline finalised a decision that led to a change of alternate destination, as inappropriate. Consequently, both the American pilot and the Korean controller were evaluated as inexperienced in dealing with such abnormal situations. These evaluations reveal that expertise and experience influence communication efficiency, including when to initiate contact and what information to convey. Another study by Kim (2018) of a different abnormal situation further demonstrates that experience and expertise significantly affect the success or failure of managing such events.

The recording analysed in Kim (2018) involved a Russian pilot from Vladivostok airlines flying from Pattaya, Thailand to Incheon, Korea, and a Korean controller. Six experienced Korean pilots and controllers served as informants. The Russian pilot requested a diversion to home country due to a technical problem, requiring the controller to coordinate controllers in North Korea and Russia. Although the Russian pilot was evaluated as having limited English proficiency, his strategy of listing the proposed alternate route was highly praised by the informants. This effort, however, proved futile, as the Korean controller was unfamiliar with air routes to neighbouring countries. The controller's continued use of plain English phrases, such as *let me know . . .*, *I want to know exact route of flight . . .*, *what's the name of fix* (fix: geographical point) or *let me check and see and call you again* (which could have been replaced with standard phraseology 'standby'), did not facilitate the Russian pilot's immediate comprehension of the messages. Most notably, the informants noted the ambiguity of the controller's language; for example, the phrase *what's the name of fix* was unclear because the controller did not specify whether he was asking for the geographical point of the airway or the point the aircraft would take after using the named airway. This ambiguity, the informants explained, stemmed from the controller's lack of knowledge of air routes and his unpreparedness to manage such an abnormal situation. The informants further observed that the controller's use of general English was intended to be recognised 'superficially and falsely, as competent' (pp. 416–417), as one informant noted. Furthermore, the informants criticised the controller's enquiry concerning a fuel issue, not because the question itself was inappropriate, but because it was posed without first clarifying and resolving the air routes, which were the priority for both parties. Despite the extended twenty-six turns regarding the air route, it remained unconfirmed until the end of transmission, leaving confirmation to the pilot in North Korean airspace. This reflects professional unreadiness, demonstrated by a lack of necessary knowledge for the controller's role and an inability to prioritise among competing issues, all of which undermine communication efficiency.

In addition to the controller's lack of professional knowledge, his habitual misuse of terms such as *affirm* (meaning 'yes'), *roger* (meaning 'I have received all of your last transmission'), or *wilco* (meaning 'I understand your message and will comply with it') – using them without fully understanding the pilot–, his noncompliance with radiotelephony conventions, specifically failing to confirm the route listed by the pilot, and his inability to rephrase questions when the pilot did not understand were identified as factors contributing to the Russian pilot's difficulties.

One final abnormal situation involved a runway incursion between a French pilot and a Korean controller, attributed to the influence of L1 phonology on the production and comprehension of instructions, combined with contextual factors, as discussed in Kim and Billington (2018). Six experienced aviation specialists provided their evaluations of this incident. Specifically, during the turn in which the Korean controller instructed the French pilot to move slightly towards the holding position during the departure phase, the instruction *Air France 267, taxi forward and hold short 16* was given. However, the French pilot's readback was *position and hold runway 16, Air France 267*. The phrase *position and hold*, developed by the Federal Aviation Administration in the US to mean 'taxi onto runway and wait on the runway', is no longer recognised as standard phraseology by ICAO. Consequently, although the controller intended for the pilot to wait on the taxiway and hold position, the pilot interpreted the instruction to taxi onto the runway, leading to a runway incursion. The informants provided evaluations on three aspects. First, they identified the pilot's incorrect readback and the controller's failure to detect it, constituting noncompliance with radiotelephony conventions. Second, the informants noted that contextual factors likely influenced the pilot's expectations. Specifically, the pilot had been informed by the controller that their take-off time would be 51 minutes, which was confirmed in previous exchanges. Hearing the instruction near 50 minutes may have led the pilot to interpret it as clearance to enter the runway. The informants observed that both the controller and pilot heard what they expected to hear, resulting in the controller not correcting the readback and the pilot entering the runway. Third, regarding linguistic challenges, the informants highlighted the difficulty Korean speakers face distinguishing between the sounds of [f] and [p]. They suggested that the [f] in *forward* within the controller's instruction was likely perceived as [p] by the pilot, causing the pilot to repeat the phrase as *position and hold*.

Building on the third aspect identified by the informants, Kim and Billington (2018) conducted an acoustic analysis using Praat. Their results suggest that substitution of [p] for [f] was unlikely to have caused the misinterpretation. However, the controller's pronunciation of *taxi* [tʰeɛɪ], which differs from pronunciations in other more common English varieties, may have been perceived by the French pilot as the final two syllables of the word *position* (e.g., [pəˈzɪʃən] in American English). Additionally, the controller pronounced *forward* as [fɔlwɜɹdə], with the final consonant of the first syllable realised as retroflex lateral [ɭ] rather than the approximant rhotic [ɹ], a common feature of Korean phonology. The controller's pronunciation also exhibited characteristics similar to those found in various English pronunciations of *hold* (e.g., [hoʊld] in American English). Thus, L1 phonological influences clearly affected both the production and perception of the relevant exchanges. Based on these analysis and findings, Kim and Billington (2018) recommend that all pilots and controllers be aware of the features of their L1 phonology that could affect their speech productions and develop appropriate strategies to enhance intelligibility in radiotelephony communication (see also Section 2.3.4).

The four studies discussed previously demonstrate that understanding radiotelephony communication requires considering multiple interconnected factors, including situational context, experience and expertise, behavioural motives (or strategy adoption), and language-related aspects such as English proficiency and L1 phonology. As with routine radiotelephony communication discussed in the previous section, compliance with radiotelephony conventions is prioritised irrespective of L1 backgrounds, not only because it is required, but because it clarifies communication and allows mutual understanding to be confirmed within systematised conventions. However, some English L1 and proficient L2+ pilots and controllers use plain English that is insufficiently concise, clear, and direct, which can hinder safe and efficient communication. One Australian controller informant highlighted the importance of standard phraseology use, noting that '[t]here is a high chance of misunderstanding, irrespective of the proficiency in English of either person . . . the use of plain language in a scenario has a likelihood of creating errors' (Kim & Friginal, 2026). Similarly, a Korean informant remarked on the American pilot's habitual general English, stating '[t]his pilot speaks English very well but he is not the one who does well in air traffic communication' (Kim & Elder, 2009, p. 23.11). The importance of adhering to standard phraseology and radiotelephony conventions is emphasised throughout the literature. However, this is not always realised in practice due to differing individual perceptions and more critically, ICAO's emphasis on English proficiency in a general sense (see Section 3.1 for details), which has reinforced the misconception that 'native' or 'native-like' proficiency represents expert competence in radiotelephony communication.

To manage the variations that inevitably arise in radiotelephony communication – such as differing levels of English proficiency, experience and expertise, and various accents – accommodation skills are essential. These skills are primarily developed through practice with both English L1 and L2+ individuals, often with more experienced seniors who recognise the value of collaborative effort for successful communication. However, current ICAO policy places responsibility solely on L2+ pilots and controllers to improve their general English proficiency, while disregarding the contributions that English L1 pilots and controllers can and should make. This approach increases the risk of unsafe and inefficient communication. Raising awareness of the importance of actively developing accommodation skills is urgent, and incorporating targeted training would significantly enhance air safety. Currently, no formal training exists; the global industry relies mainly on experienced individuals to mentor junior members within communities of practice. Insights can be gained by turning to accommodation research in ELF in other contexts, which will be discussed next.

2.3.4 Accommodation to Narrow Gaps in Unshared Repertoires: Insights from ELF Research in Other Contexts

ELF is a growing area of research, and accommodation is recognised as a core skill in ELF communication contexts (e.g., Jenkins, 2022; Kim & Penry Williams, 2021; Seidlhofer, 2009). As briefly described in Section 2, interactants introduce variation into interactions through their own linguistic and strategic repertoires, shaped by their communication experiences and practices. Sensitivity to such variation, as well as the ability to adjust one's language to align with others, is therefore essential. This process, known as accommodation, originates from Communication Accommodation Theory (Giles, 2016; Giles et al., 1991). Three strategic concepts involve accommodation: *convergence*, *divergence*, and *maintenance*. Convergence involves speakers adjusting their communicative behaviours to more closely align with their interlocutors, while divergence entails becoming more dissimilar to the interlocutor and maintenance involves retaining one's original communicative behaviours without adjustment (Dragojevic et al., 2016).

Early studies on accommodation are found exclusively in L1 communication, focussing on affective motives related to retaining or projecting identity. For example, a classic study by Bourhis and Giles (1977) demonstrates that Welsh-born English speakers who were genuinely motivated to learn Welsh converged towards an English speaker with Received Pronunciation during normal communication. However, when the English speaker made dismissive comments about the Welsh language, they diverged in both accent and content to assert their Welsh identity. Speaker attitudes towards perceived prestigious varieties also influence accommodation choices. Chakrani's (2015) study in a US diasporic setting examined five speakers of different Arab varieties. Sudanese and Moroccan Arabic speakers, whose varieties were perceived as less prestigious, accommodated more towards Saudi, Jordanian, and Egyptian Arabic speakers, whose varieties were considered more prestigious. This accommodation involved adopting various phonological and syntactic forms. The author noted that Sudanese and Moroccan speakers were expected to accommodate based on stereotypes and perceived status hierarchies. However, when the Egyptian speaker expressed negative attitudes towards the Moroccan variety, the Moroccan speaker explicitly diverged by adopting Moroccan expressions.

This, in turn, influenced the Sudanese speaker – another representative of a less prestigious variety – who displayed aversion through facial expressions and interruptions, even as he linguistically converged towards the Egyptian speaker. Thus, the perceived prestige of a variety (e.g., Received Pronunciation or certain Arab varieties) influences speaker accommodation, but speakers may also seek to preserve their linguistic identity. The role of perceived or assigned prestige in accommodation is particularly relevant to pilot-controller interactions, especially with regard to presumed competence of 'native speakers' in radiotelephony communication as designated by ICAO, which places 'native speakers' at the highest expert level and exempts them from testing, as previously mentioned. As a result of this tacit power dynamic, some L2+ pilots and controllers feel obliged to accommodate their English L1 counterparts when the latter use not only plain but also colloquial English (see Sections 4 and 5 for further discussion).

Research on accommodation in ELF has primarily focussed on cognitively motivated convergence strategies related to comprehension and communicative efficiency. This review examines studies of ELF interactions that offer insights relevant to aviation ELF in radiotelephony communication. In an early study, House (2003) recorded a half-hour group discussion between Chinese, German, Korean, and Indonesian students at a university in Germany. Analysis revealed that participants, especially the Asian students, repeated parts of others' utterances, facilitating processing and reflecting politeness. Solidarity and consensus orientation were also evident through concordant responses such as *yes*. Notably, the German student rejected the consensus-oriented 'Asian style', preferring to maintain her German communication style. In other words, she employed a maintenance strategy to preserve her German identity in communication, although House did not frame this in terms of accommodation. Cogo (2009) observed similar repetition, specifically referring to these as accommodation strategies. She examined the casual interactions of four foreign language teachers in non-classroom settings at a tertiary education institution. The study found that interlocutors' repetition of parts of their conversational partners' utterances served as a collaborative strategy, acknowledging understanding, confirming statements, and demonstrating alignment and solidarity within the same community of practice. This was evidenced by overlaps, latching (i.e., no gap between speakers' turns), and repetitions.

Focussing on how shared understanding is achieved in an ELF academic context, Kaur's (2009) study demonstrates how interlocutors collaboratively and through negotiation contribute to mutual understanding by adopting strategies such as repetition, paraphrase, and various forms of confirmation and clarification, initiated by both speakers and recipients as they monitor each other's comprehension. Problems of understanding are sometimes resolved jointly and at other times pre-emptively through proactive measures. This is possible because participants are acutely aware of the diverse linguistic backgrounds and capabilities present, leading to increased efforts from both parties. In addition to these strategies, Gaete (2022) identified completing an interlocutor's utterance as collaborative behaviour; Birlik and Kaur (2020) highlighted the important role of nonverbal strategies, such as nodding and hand-pointing gestures, in contextualising or enhancing verbal input and making understanding visible; and Kaur and Birlik (2021) noted the provision of unsolicited explanations to clarify and improve shared knowledge. While the usefulness of nonverbal strategies recalls the environmental challenges of radiotelephony communication discussed in Section 2.3.1, these findings offer valuable insights for the aviation ELF context, as assigning blame for non-understanding or misunderstanding to only one party is not meaningful in ELF interactions. Furthermore, determining what additional information would aid clarification is closely linked to domain knowledge, while effective delivery of this information depends on experience within the international aviation ELF context.

Creative meaning-making within context and openness to variation among interlocutors are also noteworthy features of interaction. In Seidlhofer's (2009) study, which involved student representatives from European universities discussing joint degree programs, a French student's phrase *endangered field* was creatively adopted and adapted by Croatian, French, and Swedish students (e.g., *endangered programs, endangered disciplines*, and *endangered activities*) to effectively communicate the concept of being at risk as it emerged from their interactions. This acceptance of the creative – or, to some users, awkward – use of the collocation, and the subsequent adoption of these variations, is significant in terms of the participants' desire to build rapport and maintain conversational flow in the situated context, rather than correcting the awkward usage through, for instance, recasting in subsequent turns. Similarly, in Pitzl's (2009) study of a business meeting, creative use of idioms and metaphors was observed. When a Korean company unknowingly distributed a copyrighted image, a German participant used the phrase *we should not wake up any dogs*, a direct translation of the German idiom 'schlafende Hunde soll man nicht wecken' (equivalent to 'let sleeping dogs lie' in English), to suggest avoiding further action. This creative expression was successfully understood by all interlocutors, demonstrating effective intercultural communication. These observations reveal that attentiveness to interlocutors' repertoires, including multilinguals' L1s, and collaborative efforts to make sense of them can contribute to shared understanding as well as foster appreciation of multicultural ELF contexts.

Regarding intelligibility in ELF contexts, Jenkins (2000) identified key phonological features for intelligibility and proposed the Lingua Franca Core. She (2000, 2007) also emphasised that the speakers' ability to accommodate their pronunciation to interlocutors is crucial in ELF communication. Some scholars (e.g., Gibbon, 2005) argue that, due to the diverse influences of L1 phonologies on production, a universal set of phonological features intelligible to all speakers in ELF contexts is unlikely. Indeed, the case study by Kim and Billington (2018), summarised earlier, found that word-final consonant clusters, vowel quality, and pitch movement – which are not included in the Lingua Franca Core – contributed to miscommunication leading to a runway incursion. Nevertheless, the Lingua Franca Core has pedagogical value, as it enables the prioritisation of specific features to enhance the efficiency and effectiveness of practice. When influential L1 phonological aspects are regularly shared within pilots' and controllers' local community as part of their everyday practice – through conversations, experiences, and specific anecdotes – radiotelephony communication can benefit greatly.

One notable ELF study that adopts the concept of a community of practice is Ehrenreich (2010), which situates its analysis within a business context. The study demonstrates how the history of long-term mutual engagement between interactants influences communication during a 90-second phone conversation. When a German project manager received an update from a Chinese sales manager, the latter's mix up between two projects was neither corrected nor clarified, yet no misunderstanding occurred, as the German manager correctly inferred what was meant. From their perspective, no issue required resolution. This suggests that a long-standing relationship can itself resolve potential confusion. Additionally, when the author asked the German manager for assistance in transcribing and comprehending the Chinese manager's utterances, the German manager explained that, although he understood the intended meaning, he could not repeat his colleague's words verbatim. This highlights how established relationships within a community of practice contribute to both spoken and unspoken communication, including intelligibility and understanding.

In light of the review of ELF research in other contexts, one significant contribution warrants particular emphasis. Supported by evidence from naturally occurring interactions, ELF research offers the potential to reconceptualise communicative competence in diverse ELF contexts. Rather than focussing on individual linguistic ability, competence within ELF is now understood as co-constructed and collaborative. Against the backdrop of shared and unshared repertoires in aviation communication, as well as the essential accommodation skills required in the international aviation ELF setting, the next section examines ICAO's decision to require 'non-native' pilots and controllers to pass an English proficiency test, along with the justification for this requirement.

3 International Civil Aviation Organisation and English Proficiency Requirements

To justify English proficiency testing requirements for 'non-native' L2+ pilots and controllers, relevant ICAO manuals (ICAO, 2004, 2010) present four examples of accidents in which, according to ICAO, investigators found that insufficient English proficiency on the part of L2+ flight crews or controllers was a contributing factor in the chain of events leading to the accidents. Additionally, the first edition of the manual (ICAO, 2004) identifies three distinct roles that language played in past accidents and incidents: (1) incorrect use of standardised phraseology, (2) lack of plain language proficiency, and (3) the use of more than one language in the same airspace. Regarding the first role, the second edition of the manual (ICAO, 2010) emphasises the significant role of standard phraseology supported by evidence from a study by Mell (1992), which reported that 70 per cent of all speech acts uttered by English L1 and L2+ pilots and controllers were not compliant with standard phraseology. The second aspect is directly related to the rationale behind the language proficiency requirements, which will be examined more closely in the following section. The third aspect concerns the use of languages normally spoken on the ground (e.g., Korean in Korean airspace); however, as English functions as a global lingua franca, it should be available for communication (ICAO, 2016). The ICAO language proficiency requirements apply to any language used for radiotelephony communication in international operations. Nevertheless, it is reasonable to assume that individual pilots and controllers are proficient L1 speakers of at least one language, typically the language spoken on the ground. Consequently, the language proficiency requirements are generally regarded as English proficiency requirements or testing policy, with the plain language referred to by L2+ pilots and controllers being plain English.

3.1 ICAO English Proficiency Requirements

As introduced earlier, there are six assessment criteria across six levels, with the descriptors for the highest expert level 6 shown in Table 1. In a previous paper, I (Kim, 2024) critiqued the assessment criteria and rating scale, noting that the specific linguistic characteristics of radiotelephony communication are not at all reflected in them.

In brief, *pronunciation* and *comprehension* emphasise ease and accuracy of understanding, treating L1-influenced pronunciations as speaker deficiencies rather than as indicators of respondents' competence, thereby leaving no room for negotiation between interlocutors. Moreover, by exempting 'native

Table 1 Descriptors for expert level 6 in six assessment criteria (ICAO, 2004, 2010)

Assessment criteria	Descriptors
Pronunciation	Pronunciation, stress, rhythm, and intonation, though possibly influenced by the first language or regional variation, almost never interfere with ease of understanding.
Structure	Both basic and complex grammatical structures and sentence patterns are consistently well controlled.
Vocabulary	Vocabulary range and accuracy are sufficient to communicate effectively on a wide variety of familiar and unfamiliar topics. Vocabulary is idiomatic, nuanced, and sensitive to register.
Fluency	Able to speak at length with a natural, effortless flow. Varies speech flow for stylistic effect, for example, to emphasise a point. Uses appropriate discourse markers and connectors spontaneously.
Comprehension	Comprehension is consistently accurate in nearly all contexts and includes comprehension of linguistic and cultural subtleties.
Interactions	Interacts with ease in nearly all situations. Is sensitive to verbal and non-verbal cues and responds to them appropriately.

speakers', it is assumed that their pronunciation and comprehension never pose problems. Regarding *structure* and *vocabulary*, complexity in grammatical patterns and the use of idiomatic or nuanced vocabulary are emphasised, despite these being recognised elsewhere by ICAO as impediments to radiotelephony communication. For *fluency* and *interactions*, extended speech and sensitivity to both verbal and non-verbal are highlighted, although these features can hinder or be irrelevant to effective radiotelephony communication. These ICAO descriptors have also been criticised by McNamara (2010) for being implemented solely for policy purposes and failing to reflect the target domain, and by Fulcher (2015) for lacking relevance by focussing on general *interactions*, arguing that descriptors could apply to any context.

This lack of specificity and relevance to the construct of radiotelephony communication has been further criticised by domain specialists. Knoch's

(2014) validation study of ICAO's rating scale with English L1 domain specialists, using recorded speech samples, found that *technical knowledge*, *experience*, and *training level* were the most mentioned categories by pilot experts alongside *pronunciation*. Kim and Elder's (2015) survey revealed that while the great majority of Korean pilots and controllers considered ICAO's English proficiency requirements, as they stand, to be (completely) unnecessary (69 per cent). The respondents were also negative about the test developed in Korea to meet the ICAO requirements, with 76 per cent indicating that the construct of radiotelephony communication is not well or not at all reflected in the test. Of the assessment criteria, they were particularly critical of the *structure* and *fluency* criteria. Kim and Friginal (2025) further discuss these descriptors in terms of construct under-representation and construct irrelevance. Regarding construct under-representation, linguistically valued aspects of radiotelephony communication – such as simple, concise, unambiguous messages, handling various accents, and accommodation – are absent from the rating scale. For construct irrelevance, opposing qualities that may hinder safe radiotelephony communication – such as complex grammatical patterns, idiomatic expressions, and non-verbal cues – are identified as construct irrelevant variance. Due to these shortcomings, the authors argue that the current ICAO English proficiency requirements inevitably produce negative or detrimental washback (i.e., the effect of tests on learning and teaching) for pilots and controllers.

Since the construct is defined a priori by policymakers, the test developers' 'thinking stage' (McNamara, 2010, 2011), in which evidence is gathered from the target domain and the domain is modelled, is eliminated; this results in unfair and unjust testing practices. The next section examines ICAO's justification for English proficiency requirements.

3.2 Justification for the Policy: Past Aircraft Accidents

Four aircraft accidents are examined, with the first accident analysed in more detail. This is followed by a commentary on studies of accidents for which different interpretations have been proposed. These divergent interpretations highlight the complexities inherent in aviation accidents. Factors contributing to accidents – including severe weather conditions, a loss of spatial orientation or situational awareness, visual illusions, fatigue, poor aircrew coordination, and communication errors or English proficiency deficits – are typically categorised and presented in accident investigation reports. The four accidents are summarised in Table 2.

Table 2 Four aircraft accidents widely cited by ICAO and other literature

	Accidents	Pilots	Controllers	Reasons considered
1	Runway collision at Tenerife airport, Canary Islands, 1977. 583 fatalities	Pan America (American) & KLM (Dutch)	Spanish	Interference from Dutch pilot's L1
2	Crash due to fuel exhaustion, Cove Neck, New York, the US, 1990. 73 fatalities	Avianca (Colombian)	American	Spanish pilot's failure to communicate clearly with American controller over fuel shortage
3	Crash into mountain terrain Cali, Colombia, 1995. 159 fatalities	American Airlines (American)	Colombian	Colombian controller's lack of engagement in communication
4	Mid-air collision India, 1996. 349 fatalities	Saudi Arabian Airlines (Saudi Arabian) & Kazakhstan Airlines (Kazakh)	Indian	Saudi Arabian pilots' lack of understanding of Indian controller's instructions

3.2.1 Runway Collision at Tenerife Airport, Canary Islands

Of the four accidents that ICAO cited, the runway collision at Tenerife in the Canary Islands in 1977 is the deadliest in aviation history, resulting in 583 fatalities. This accident is selected for closer analysis because it is frequently referenced as an instance where English proficiency was identified as a contributing factor, often accompanied by statements supporting the ICAO English proficiency testing policy (e.g., Alderson, 2009; Tajima, 2004).

On 27 March 1977, KLM flight 4805, bound from Amsterdam to Las Palmas de Gran Canaria, and Pan America (Pan Am) flight 1736, bound from Los Angeles via New York to Las Palmas de Gran Canaria, were diverted to Los Rodeos airport in Tenerife because their original destination was closed due to a bomb explosion in the passenger terminal. As a result of this diversion, the

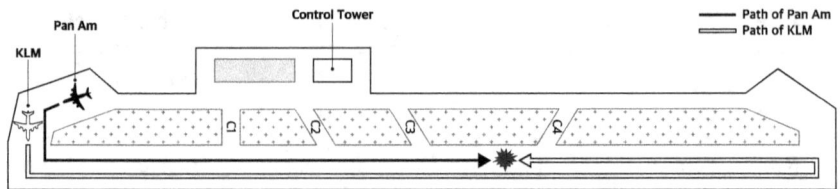

Figure 2 Illustration of the accident at Tenerife airport (Reproduced from (Roitsch et al., 1978, p. 30) with permission from the Air Line Pilots Association, International)

regional airport became congested, with five diverted aircraft occupying its limited taxiways. The Pan Am flight arrived at the airport before the KLM flight, and both aircraft were parked along the same taxiway. When Las Palmas airport finally reopened, although the Pan Am flight was ready for departure, it had to wait until the KLM aircraft was ready due to insufficient space to overtake the KLM aircraft on the same taxiway leading to the runway.

The KLM flight was eventually instructed to taxi to the end of runway, where it would perform a backtrack for its take-off run, as shown in Figure 2. Subsequently, the Pan Am flight was instructed to taxi down the same runway but to turn off at the third taxiway, C3 (see Figure 2), to the left, allowing the KLM flight to use the runway for take-off.

The transcript (ICAO, 1978, pp. 56–57) below presents the transmission immediately preceding the accident. Note that adjustments have been made to conform to the transcription conventions.

```
17:05:44.8
(1) KLM:              Uh, the KLM ... four eight zero five
                      is now ready for take-off ... uh
                      and we're waiting for our ATC
                      clearance.
17:05:53.4
(2) Controller:       KLM eight seven zero five uh you
                      are cleared to the Papa Beacon
                      climb to and maintain flight level
                      nine zero ... right turn after
                      take-off proceed with heading zero
                      four zero until intercepting
                      the three two five radial from Las
                      Palmas VOR
17:06:09.6
(3) KLM:              Ah roger sir, we're cleared to Papa
                      Beacon flight level nine zero,
```

		right turn out zero four zero until intercepting the three two five and <u>we're now ### (at take-off)</u>.
17:06:20.08	(4) Controller:	#K... [stand by for take-off, I will call you.]
17:06:20.3	(5) Pan Am Pilot:	No, uh...
	Pan Am Co-pilot:	[₂And we're still taxiing down the runway, the Clipper 1736]

In turn (1), the KLM pilot indicated readiness for take-off to the controller. In turn (2), the controller granted the KLM clearance for the airways to be taken once airborne, specifying the flight level and direction to Las Palmas. This instruction was subsequently read back by the KLM pilot in turn (3). In turn (4), the controller instructed the KLM to wait for take-off; however, this critical message was overlapped with the Pan Am co-pilot's transmission in turn (5), which indicated that they were taxiing on the runway. This overlap blocked the radio channel, preventing the instruction from reaching the KLM cockpit. Having already commenced its take-off, the KLM aircraft collided with the Pan Am aircraft on the runway.

The accident report (ICAO, 1978) indicated that the take-off run began immediately after turn (3) in the transcript. It shows that the KLM pilot was operating on the assumption that the runway had been cleared by the Pan Am aircraft, despite not having received clearance from the controller. The overlap of turns (4) and (5) was critical, as the controller's stand-by message in turn (4) might have prevented the KLM aircraft from proceeding with its take-off run if it had been heard.

Various factors were identified as causes and contributing factors in the accident report. These include a growing sense of tension, severe weather conditions, the concurrence of two transmission turns, inadequate language, and the Pan Am pilots missing the correct taxiway to exit the runway, which was necessary for the KLM flight's take-off. The report first highlighted that the mounting tension experienced by the captain of the KLM flight was likely due to his awareness of the possibility of exceeding the strict limits on duty time, which might have forced him to interrupt the flight. It was also reported that the worsening weather conditions at the airport might have exacerbated this tension. Adverse weather was identified as a contributing factor, as fog and low-lying clouds driven by wind caused reduced and rapidly changing visibility. Third, the simultaneous transmissions – turns (4) and (5) in the transcript – were described as a factor. Three additional contributing factors were also identified: the inadequate language of the KLM co-pilot; the unusual traffic congestion, which required aircraft to taxi on an active runway; and the Pan Am aircraft's failure to make a left turn at the third intersection, C3 (see Figure 2), as instructed. However, the last factor was considered less relevant because the Pan Am pilot never reported the runway as clear but instead advised that the aircraft was taxiing on it twice, including turn (5) in the transcript.

One of the contributing factors, described as 'inadequate language', drew ICAO's attention, leading to the conclusion that the KLM co-pilot's insufficient English proficiency was central to the problem. In turn (3), the KLM co-pilot stated *we are now (at take-off)*, in addition to his readback. It was reported that this utterance was not sufficiently clear to determine the exact wording but was transcribed as shown. This was considered indicative of interference from Dutch, the pilot's L1, in which the present progressive is expressed by a construction equivalent of *at* in English followed by the infinitive form of the verb. Thus, it was inferred that the pilot intended to say 'we are taking off', but this was interpreted by the controller as 'ready to take-off'.

This alleged 'interference' from the Dutch pilot's L1 was presented as an example of insufficient command of English during the second meeting of the proficiency requirements in common English study group (ICAO, 2001), which was established to assist ICAO in advancing the development of language proficiency provisions. These interpretations recognised by ICAO, though assumed, carry authoritative weight and have subsequently been accepted as verified truths. They have been cited in later research as evidence of inadequate English proficiency on the part of the Dutch pilot (Tajima, 2004), with minor words playing a significant role in the miscommunication (Campbell-Laird, 2004), and as support of the justification for requiring proficiency testings of 'non-native speakers' (Alderson, 2009; Prinzo et al., 2008). All of these explanations focus on limitations in general English use rather than on the use of standard phraseology in radiotelephony communication.

However, this same sentence has been examined from a different perspective in other studies. Philps (1991) explains that the KLM pilots' expectations may have influenced their interpretation while waiting for take-off clearance; causing them to hear what they expected to hear. This phenomenon is known as *confirmation bias* in psychology, which refers to the tendency for 'information [to be] searched for, interpreted, and remembered in such a way that it systematically impedes the possibility that the hypothesis could be rejected – that is, it fosters the immunity of the hypothesis' (Oswald & Grosjean, 2004, p. 79). Thus, the KLM pilots might have interpreted the situation as indicating that the clearance for take-off had been granted. Similarly, Hawkins and Orlady (2017) attributed the accident to a false hypothesis or mistaken assumption, whereby the pilots may have believed that they had been properly cleared for take-off – as well as to noncompliance with standard phraseology and clearance procedures. Weick (1990) and Krause (2003) interpret the Dutch pilot's utterance *we're now (at take-off)* as an instance of nonstandard phraseology, and Cushing (1995) similarly regards it as nonstandard phraseology. The standard phraseology used in this phase is initiated by a controller issuing the clearance *cleared for take-off* and the pilot must read back the message by repeating *cleared for take-off*.

The accident at Tenerife also prompted changes in standard phraseology and procedures. The Spanish government report on the accident made three key recommendations: emphasising the importance of strict compliance with instructions and clearance; using standard, concise, and unequivocal aeronautical language, and avoiding the word *take-off* (Subsecretaria de Aviacion Civil, 1978). Based on these recommendations, ICAO reviewed the relevant phraseology and procedures, with the resulting amendments becoming effective in 1984. The most notable change was the restriction on the use of the words *clear* or *clearance* and *take-off*, both of which had been used in turn (2). Although the transcript clearly shows that the clearance referred only to the airways the KLM flight would follow after becoming airborne and that the word *take-off* in this context did not pertain to the actual take-off procedure, it was considered potentially confusing for pilots, as demonstrated by the Tenerife accident. Consequently, following the amendments, the word *clear/clearance* was replaced by more specific terms such as *start-up*, *push-back*, and *taxi*, while *take-off* was replaced by *depart* or *departure*, except when referring to the actual take-off itself (Hawkins & Orlady, 2017). These changes suggest that the cause of the accident was perceived to be due at least in part to ambiguity in the phraseology repertoire, rather than the pilot's limited English proficiency, as ICAO has assumed and argued.

3.2.2 Crash Due to Fuel Starvation over New York, the US

Contrary interpretations of the role of English emerge in analyses of a second aircraft accident: the 1990 Avianca flight crash caused by fuel exhaustion at Cove Neck, New York. Operated by the Colombian airline Avianca, the flight from Medellin, Colombia to New York experienced delays totalling approximately 1 hour and 17 minutes due to poor weather en route to John F. Kennedy airport. To convey the urgency of the fuel emergency, the first officer repeatedly informed the American controllers in the approach and tower sectors, stating phrases such as *we need priority*, *we'll be able to hold about five minutes that's all we can do*, *we run out of fuel now*, and *once again we're running out of fuel*. The captain instructed the first officer in Spanish to emphasise their emergency status, including after a missed approach caused by runway invisibility. The first officer's final message before acknowledging the controller's instruction was *we just ah lost two engines and ah we need priority please*, followed by further cockpit communication between the captain and first officer. The aircraft ultimately crashed into a forested residential hillside on the north shore of Long Island, resulting in 73 fatalities.

The accident report (NTSB, 1991) identified the probable causes as the flight crew's failure to manage fuel properly and to communicate the emergency fuel situation to the controllers before fuel exhaustion. Contributing factors included the crew's failure to use the airline's dispatch system during an international flight into a busy airport under poor weather conditions, inadequate traffic flow management by the Federal Aviation Administration, and the lack of standardised, clear terminology between the pilots and the controllers regarding minimum and emergency fuel states.

ICAO (2004) identified this language use as an example of insufficient English on the part of the Colombian Spanish-speaking pilot. Similarly, Tajima (2004) argued that the accident could have been prevented if the Colombian pilot had possessed adequate English skills. Alderson (2009), in support of the ICAO testing policy, highlighted both the pilot's failure to communicate clearly and the controllers' lack of effective communication strategies. While acknowledging limited English proficiency as a factor, Orasanu (1994) noted that the captain and first officer did not share a mutual understanding of the severity of the fuel problem. Specifically, the captain repeatedly confirmed with the first officer, in Spanish, that the emergency situation had been communicated to the controllers, to which the first officer responded affirmatively; however, the first officer's actual messages to the controllers failed to convey the urgency of the situation.

Interestingly, opposing interpretations of the language use in this situation have been presented in other studies. In his analysis of the accident, Helmreich (1994) argued that the Colombian pilot's offhand request for priority, delivered in excellent, unaccented, monotone English, misled the controllers. He suggested that the pilot's failure to follow procedures, specifically, not declaring an emergency (i.e., using *mayday*) reduced the controllers' sense of urgency. Krause (2003) described this language use as nonstandard phraseology, while Cushing (1994) characterised it as the use of an English phrase rather than a technical aviation term. This highlights how different analyses of the same instance of language use can yield multiple interpretations of the contributing factors.

3.2.3 Crash into Mountain Terrain in Cali, Colombia

In this accident, language use as shown in the transcript did not emerge as an issue in the analysis of discourse between the American pilot and the

Colombian, Spanish-speaking controller. Differences in evaluating or understanding the contributors' behaviours were based on argument rather than direct evidence. American Airlines flight 965, en route from Miami to Alfonso Bonilla Aragón airport in Cali, Colombia, crashed into mountainous terrain in 1995, leading to the loss of 159 lives. The controller at Cali Approach proposed a different runway than initially planned, which the American Airlines captain accepted. Realising limited time to execute the new approach, the captain requested clearance to proceed to the beacon known as ROZO, which the controller approved. However, when the pilot entered R into the flight management system, it selected a different beacon named ROMEO, located near Bogotá, 130 miles away (see Figure 3). Later, when the captain and the first officer realised they were off course, they struggled to determine their location and further lost awareness of their distance from terrain, indicating a loss of positional situational awareness and triggering the ground proximity warning system (Endsley & Strauch, 1997). An attempted climb failed because the speed brake had been applied, preventing ascent. These factors ultimately caused the crash.

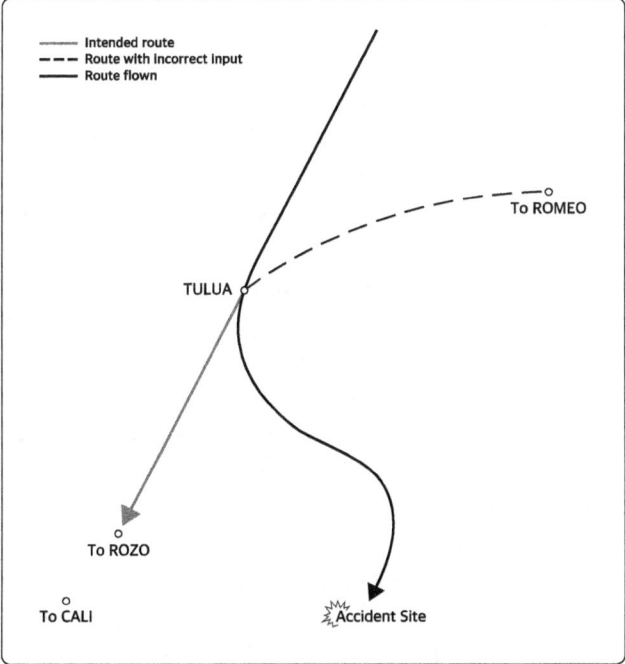

Figure 3 Illustration of the accident in Cali (Simplified from NTSB (n.d.), with permission from The Boeing Company)

Like other accidents, this one had multiple probable causes. The official investigation report by Colombia (Aeronautica Civil of the Republic of Colombia, 1996) identified pilot errors during several execution phases and a loss of situational awareness. Endsley and Strauch (1997) and Strauch (1997) note that reliance on the flight management system – designed to enhance situation awareness and reduce workload – can adversely affect both, emphasising the critical importance of situational awareness in the effective planning and execution of instrument approaches. The accident report also highlighted differing views on the Colombian controller's role, seemingly influenced by the interests of each party. The report noted that, due to the lack of radar coverage, the controller relied entirely on pilot-provided information. Deficiencies in this information contributed to the controller's lack of awareness, compounded by inadequate training in soliciting information from the pilots to identify their difficulties. In fact, the report stated that the controller's English proficiency was insufficient to address the inconsistencies between the perceived and actual locations of the aircraft. In this context, American Airlines argued that the controller's English was inadequate (Simmon, 1998), and ICAO suggested the controller could have taken a more active communicative role. Tajima (2004) went so far as to argue that better English proficiency might have prevented the accident, though no evidence supported this claim.

However, of the twenty-seven errors identified in Simmon's (1998) analysis, only two were related to language use, both involving standard phraseology and radiotelephony compliance. One concerned the controller's nonstandard phraseology when issuing clearance and the pilot's incorrect readback; the other involved the controller's failure to correct the pilot's incorrect readback, which contributed to the pilot's confirmation bias and caused them to believe they were correct, as previously explained in the accident at Tenerife. Among numerous recommendations to the Federal Aviation Administration, ICAO, and American Airlines, the Colombian report emphasised strict adherence to ICAO standard phraseology and terminology in radiotelephony communication. The accident report by Colombia (1996) states that, in the initial interview, the controller reported no communication difficulties with the pilot. However, in a subsequent interview, when asked about L1 differences, he indicated that he would have probed more deeply if there had been no limitation in his command of English. ICAO and others cited this as unequivocal evidence, stating that 'by his own admission' (Friginal et al., 2019, p. 11; ICAO, 2004, p. 7–2), the controller lacked

English proficiency. It is highly inappropriate to use the confession of the second victim – who was involved in an accident that resulted in the death of 159 people and was, in all likelihood, experiencing fear, guilt, and distress over both the accident and his perceived failures (Dekker, 2013) – to justify policy decisions by emphasising what he could or should have done, or the skills he ought to have possessed. Dekker further argues that such an approach risks inducing shame and undermining the second victim's professional identity and warns that accident investigations are intended as reviews of events for organisational and structural learning, not as individual performance reviews designed to locate blame.

3.2.4 Midair Collision over Charkhi Dadri, India

The last accident involved communication between a radio operator in the cockpit – not a captain or a first officer – and a controller. In 1996, a midair collision between Kazakhstan Airlines flight 1907 and Saudi Arabian Airlines flight 736 over Charkhi Dadri, India, resulted in 349 fatalities. The Kazakh flight was inbound from Kazakhstan to New Delhi, while the Saudi Arabian flight was outbound from New Delhi to Saudi Arabia. The New Delhi controller assigned an altitude of 15,000 feet to the Kazakh aircraft and 14,000 feet to the Saudi Arabian aircraft to maintain vertical separation. However, the Kazakh aircraft descended to 14,000 feet and collided with the Saudi Arabian aircraft.

Unlike other accidents with publicly available official reports, the investigation results for this collision are not accessible. The probable cause was reported as the unauthorised descent by the Kazakh aircraft and its failure to maintain the assigned altitude of 15,000 feet (Aviation Safety Network, n.d.). Given that the Kazakh aircraft was flying at 14,500 feet when the radio operator reported reaching 15,000 feet, followed by a further 310-foot descent, miscommunication between the radio operator and the cockpit pilots is likely. A critical aspect of the communication was the controller's warning to the Kazakh flight about the Saudi aircraft's position: *Roger, maintain 150, identified traffic 12 o'clock, reciprocal Saudi Boeing 747, 14 miles, report in sight*. When the radio operator requested the distance again, the controller replied *14 miles now, roger, 1907*. No response followed, prompting the controller to restate *Traffic in 13 miles, level 140*. It is plausible that the Kazakh pilots, not directly engaged in communication, misinterpreted the traffic information as an instruction rather than a warning.

Similar to the accident in Cali, Delhi airport lacked secondary surveillance radar at the time, preventing controllers from monitoring aircraft altitude and forcing them to rely on crew-reported information. Consequently, the controller was unaware that the Kazakh aircraft was flying below its assigned altitude. Following the accident, guidelines emphasised direct communication between pilots and controllers, particularly in approach control, to minimise time lag (Government of India Civil Aviation Department, 1999). Media reports attributed the accident to the Kazakh crew's limited English proficiency. While multiple languages are common in international airspace, Alderson (2009) identified the involvement of three different L1s in this case as a potential source of confusion. Similarly, Tajima (2004) attributed the accident to inadequate English proficiency of the Kazakh crew.

3.3 Reduced Complexities

The first two accidents – the runway collision at Tenerife airport and the fuel exhaustion crash over New York – were analysed from two different perspectives: compliance with standard phraseology in radiotelephony communication and English proficiency. Although ICAO regulations prioritise compliance with standard phraseology over other language conventions, analyses of these incidents often emphasise English proficiency, which can obscure issues of non-compliance. In the third accident, the collision with mountain terrain in Cali, Colombia, the transcript showed no clear signs of English proficiency. However, some scholars attributed the controller's passivity or lack of further engagement in communication to limited proficiency. In the last accident, the midair collision over Charkhi Dadri, India, some miscommunication between the radio operator and the pilots in the cockpit may be inferred. Yet, since communication occurred in Kazakh, their first language, it is unreasonable to attribute miscommunication to English proficiency.

Although accident investigations reveal numerous intertwined factors embedded throughout the events and literature reflects varying focusses, ICAO's emphasis on English proficiency – along with hindsight-based suggestions involving numerous 'ifs' – is not only misleading but also obscures the full complexity of the accidents. This single-factor bias prevents a comprehensive understanding of the accidents as outcomes emerging from the interaction of multiple factors, from the complexity perspective (Cilliers, 2005; Dekker et al., 2011). The common practice of classifying human errors into discrete categories has also been criticised. Angell and Straub (1999) argue that such categories are misleading because they fail to capture the complexity of actual practice. Similarly, Dekker (2003) warns of the dangers inherent in classifying human errors:

> Error classification disembodies data. It removes the context that helped produce the error in its particular manifestation. This disables understanding because by excising performance fragments away from their context, error classification destroys the local rationality principle. (p. 98)

Furthermore, Dekker (2001) criticises prevailing investigative practices for relying predominantly on voice recording data, which focus on the individual responsible for the failure, the actions they could have taken to prevent the outcome, and how they failed to act or notice critical information. All alleged causes are identified with the benefit of hindsight. Dekker emphasises that voice recordings provide only a partial record of events, and human performance is context-dependent; thus, meaningful analysis requires detailed contextual information. He also suggests reconsidering ICAO Annex 13, which designates voice recordings as a primary source for accident investigation. Hawkins and Orlady (2017) points out that continuous monitoring of communication aspects, with changes implemented when necessary, is required. It is also the responsibility of ICAO to consider more standardised communication procedures for abnormal situations in radiotelephony.

There is a paucity of research on the use of plain English in radiotelephony communication, with most studies relying primarily on transcripts of rare past accidents. This focus may stem from the fact that plain English is not commonly expected in radiotelephony communication, except when criticising noncompliant behaviours in situations where colloquial English is used, even though standard phraseology would suffice. Emphasising accidents as the primary context for analysis may also reflect limited access to less extreme but more frequently occurring – and potentially informative – situations. In this regard, examining naturally occurring performance in abnormal situations offers valuable insights, as reviewed in Section 2.3.3. The following section provides an example of such an analysis.

4 Discourse Analysis and Domain Specialists' Evaluations

The discourse presented in this section is part of a larger study (Kim, 2012) involving six naturally occurring, audio-recorded live discourse samples. One of these examples is analysed in this section, drawing on insights from domain specialists. After the methods and analysis are explained, the discourse is presented with contextual information from aviation specialists in Section 4.2. The aviation specialists' evaluations and interpretations of the event and performance in the recording are then presented in Section 4.3.

4.1 Methods

The research builds on *grounded theory* (Strauss & Corbin, 1994), specifically employing *grounded ethnography*, an approach to 'describing and understanding a target language use situation from the perspective of language users in that situation' (Douglas, 2000, p. 93). The relevant discourse serves as the primary data source and is used as a stimulus, while the perspectives of aviation specialist informants constitute the second data source. Jacoby and McNamara (1999) use the term 'indigenous' assessment to identify the underlying values in domain specialists' judgements, focussing on the criteria the professional members use for their socialisation and assessment practices.

4.1.1 Discourse Analysis

The associated discourse was collected from Incheon Control Tower in Korea, which manages aircraft operations at and around the aerodrome. The episode involves a towing request from the runway due to an aircraft's hydraulic failure. Four participants are featured in the recording: an Australian pilot and three Korean controllers, with each controller replaced by another with better English proficiency. I initially attempted to transcribe the discourse with assistance from one controller informant; however, the majority of the transcription was completed during a focus group workshop with controller informants.

4.1.2 Eliciting Aviation Specialists' Perspectives

To gather domain specialists' perspectives on the performance in the discourse, six aviation experts were recruited: three Korean pilots with 13, 13, and 14 years of experience and three Korean controllers with 20, 21, and 23 years of experience, respectively. Individual workshops were conducted with the pilot informants, while a focus group workshop was held with the controller informants. For the relevant episode, workshop durations ranged from 50 minutes to 1 hour and 5 minutes for the pilots and 2 hours 10 minutes for the controllers. The informants were provided with the transcript of the discourse and listened to the audio recording. They were asked to comment on five aspects: (1) the Australian pilot's overall professionalism in handling the situation; (2) the three Korean controllers' overall professionalism in handling the situation; (3) the appropriateness of both standard phraseology and the use of plain English; (4) their personal experience of similar situations; and (5) their personal recommendations for effective communication in similar situations. All workshops were conducted in Korean, the L1 of both the informants and the author and were audio-recorded in their entirety.

4.1.3 Analysis of Workshops with Aviation Specialists

The audio-recorded workshops were transcribed, translated into English, and analysed thematically. Thematic analysis is a method for identifying themes or patterns within data (Braun & Clarke, 2006). Braun and Clarke note that thematic analysis can adopt an essentialist or realist approach, focussing on the semantic meanings of participants' statements, or a constructionist approach, focussing on latent aspects such as the influence of community or societal discourse. In this study, I primarily focussed on semantic meanings, while also considering latent aspects where relevant. Themes were developed and revised during multiple passes through the transcripts.

Table 3 summarises the themes developed for coding. The two main superordinate themes, DOMAIN ASPECTS and LANGUAGE ASPECTS, shown in small capitals, are directly related to performance in the recording and to the informants' experience in radiotelephony communication. Each comprises relevant subordinate themes, which are indicated by single quotation marks in the text, sometimes in varied forms (e.g., 'accommodation' as 'accommodate'). The

Table 3 Themes developed for coding

Superordinate themes	Subordinate themes
DOMAIN ASPECTS	• Professional knowledge • Professional competence • Experience • Other
LANGUAGE ASPECTS	• Accommodation • Speech rate • Comprehension • Vocabulary • Plain English • English proficiency • Intelligibility • Accent familiarity • Local accents • Message markers • Inadequacy of existing standard phraseology and radiotelephony conventions • Other
OTHER	• ICAO English proficiency requirements • Review of transcript and context

coding process revealed that these two aspects were often intertwined in the informants' commentaries; for example, certain verbal outputs were attributed to a lack of knowledge. However, for analytical purposes and to highlight distinct aspects of this professional setting, domain-specific themes, including the use of standard phraseology, were grouped under DOMAIN ASPECTS, while language-specific themes were grouped under LANGUAGE ASPECTS. As previously noted, compliance with standard phraseology and radiotelephony conventions (e.g., readback and hearback) is recognised in the literature as a key professional protocol; therefore, it was coded under 'professional competence' within the DOMAIN ASPECTS superordinate theme.

During the workshops, although not directly relevant to performance in the discourse or to the informants' related experience – and thus categorised under the superordinate theme OTHER – discussions naturally led to an evaluation of ICAO English proficiency requirements. Additionally, particularly during the focus group workshop with the controller informants, substantial time was devoted to reviewing the transcript of the Australian pilot's turns and having the informants explain the context; this was coded as 'review of transcript and context'.

4.2 Radiotelephony Discourse

An Australian pilot of Cathay 416 – the flight identification – is on the radio, flying into Incheon international airport from Hong Kong. Immediately after being handed over from Seoul Approach, which manages aircraft arriving at or departing from the airport, to the airport tower, which manages aircraft on the aerodrome, the pilot informs the first Korean controller that the aircraft will be stopping on the runway due to a steering problem caused by hydraulic system failure.

The discourse is lengthy, but I have chosen to present it in full to take advantage of the space this monograph provides and to illustrate the complexity of an abnormal situation in this high-stakes field. The transmission is divided into three parts based on each controller's involvement and lasts 19 minutes and 37 seconds, comprising 122 turns in total. The first controller is involved in turns 1 to 22 (18 per cent of the discourse), the second controller in turns 23 to 56 (28 per cent), and the third controller in turns 57 to 122 (54 per cent). Technical terms are explained in footnotes. Transmissions between the first controller and other aircraft in Part One are indicated as transcriber comments. The transcription conventions used are as follows:

. . . micropause
(1.2) silence in seconds
unintelligible
((words)) transcriber comment
A line between turns indicates a lapse, after which a new contact is made.

4.2.1 Part One with the First Controller

Cathay 416 is approaching its assigned runway. When confirming the assignment, the pilot informs the controller that the aircraft will stop on the runway.

```
<T=0.00>
(1) pilot:           Incheon Tower, Cathay 416, estab-
                     lished ILS/DME²33 Right
(2) controller:      Cathay 416, Incheon Tower, continue
                     approach runway 33 Right³
(3) pilot:           Continue approach, Cathay 416

((the controller is talking with the pilots of other air-
craft for 28 seconds))

<T=0.42>
(4) controller:      Cathay 416, wind, correction, wind
                     calm, cleared to land, runway 33
                     Right
(5) pilot:           Cleared to land, 33 Right, Cathay 416

((the controller is talking with the pilots of other
aircraft for 1 minute and 3 seconds))

<T=1.53>
(6) pilot:           Seoul Tower, Cathay 416
(7) controller:      Cathay 416, confirm, cleared to land
                     runway 33 Right
(8) pilot:           Okay, we're cleared to land 33 Right,
                     be advised we'll be stopping on the
                     runway
(9) controller:      Roger⁴

((the controller is talking with the pilots of other
aircraft for 58 seconds))
```

In turn (1), Cathay 416 provides its landing system information and confirms the assigned runway to the controller. The controller reconfirms the runway in turn (2) and provides wind information and landing clearance in turn (4). When the pilot contacts the tower in turn (6), the controller confirms the clearance in turn (7). In turn (8), the pilot repeats that clearance has been given and states that the aircraft will stop on the runway, using the phrase *be advised* to convey this

---

[2] ILS stands for Instrument Landing System. The airport transmits localiser and glide slope radio signals, enabling the aircraft to align with the runway's centreline and descent path. DME stands for Distance Measurement Equipment, which provides the distance between the runway and the aircraft.
[3] Runway 33 Right is one of three runways at Incheon international airport.
[4] Roger means 'I have received your transmission'.

information. Although the controller responds with *roger*, indicating receipt, he does not understand the pilot's message. This lack of understanding continues in subsequent turns. Meanwhile, Cathay 416 lands and contacts the tower while taxiing on the runway.

```
<T=3.09>
(10) pilot:          Incheon Tower, Cathay 416, we can be
                     advised stopping on the runway
(11) controller:     Confirm, end of runway vacated?
(12) pilot:          er, negative, negative, stopping in
                     the position our runway. We'll not be
                     clearing
(13) controller:     Roger

((the controller is talking with the pilots of other aircraft
for 20 seconds))
```

In turn (10), while the aircraft is rolling on the runway, the pilot repeats that it will be stopping on the runway. However, in turn (11), the controller requests confirmation that the aircraft can vacate the runway. The pilot clarifies the misunderstanding by responding *negative, negative* in turn (12) and reiterates that the aircraft will not be able to vacate the runway. Although the controller replies *roger*, subsequent turns indicate that he still does not understand the message.

```
<T=3.46>
(14) controller:     Cathay 416, confirm left turn taxi via
                     Charlie 4⁵, no delay
(15) pilot:          Tower, Cathay 416, negative, we've had
                     a complete draining hydraulic failure,
                     we have to maintain our position on the
                     runway, we require a tug to tow us to
                     the bay
(16) controller:               Korean Air 552, go around,
                               climb to 3 thousand, runway
                               heading
(17) pilot of Korean Air 552:  Tower, now go around
```

At this stage of the transmission, the aircraft stops on the runway. Observing this, the controller contacts the pilot in turn (14), stating that the runway must be vacated immediately. In turn (15), the pilot explains the aircraft's condition and the reason for being unable to comply. Realising there is an issue, the controller instructs Korean Air 552, which is approaching the same runway, to execute a *go around* in turn (16). This instruction is repeated by the pilot of Korean Air 552 in turn (17).

---

[5] Charlie 4 is the name of a taxiway.

Aviation English as a Global Lingua Franca

In subsequent turns, although the controller recognises that the aircraft has a problem, he does not realise it is unable to move on its own. He asks how long it will remain in its current position.

```
<T=4.15>
(18) controller:     Cathay 416, how many time your delay?
(19) pilot:          We require a tug to be towed off the
                     runway, we'll require a tug. Can you
                     arrange for a tow truck to tug off the
                     runway?
(20) controller:     Roger

((the controller is talking with the pilots of other
aircraft for 22 seconds))

<T=6.54>
(21) controller:     Cathay 416, contact 118275
(22) pilot:          118275, Cathay 416
```

In turn (18), the controller asks about the expected delay, and in turn (19), the pilot reiterates the request for a tow truck. After a minute, the controller provides a separate frequency to the pilot, ending his involvement in the exchange. With the separate frequency assigned, subsequent communication does not affect radiotelephony with other aircraft, and runway 33 Right is closed. Incheon airport has three runways, and aircraft assigned to runway 33 Right are diverted to the other ones.

4.2.2 Part Two with the Second Controller

In Part Two, the pilot and the second controller communicate regarding requests for a tow truck and a fire truck. Using a separate frequency, they interact exclusively on this new channel. The pilot reiterates the aircraft's condition and requests a tow truck. In Parts Two and Three, most communication is in rather colloquial English, except for terms such as *roger* or *affirmative*, identification phrases like *(Incheon) Ground* or *Cathay 416*, and the names of airport taxiways.

```
<T=7.12>
(23) pilot:          Incheon, Cathay 416
(24) controller:     Cathay 416

(25) pilot:          Incheon, Cathay 416
(26) controller:     Cathay 416, Incheon Ground, say your
                     condition again please
(27) pilot:          Cathay 416, we're in position on
                     runway 33 Right, we've had a er...
                     steering failure of the aircraft,
                     complete steering failure, so we
```

	are unable to taxi until we are tugged to the bay
(28) controller:	Roger that, so do you need a towing truck, right?
(29) pilot:	Ye, we need er...tugged to get all the way to the bay and be advised there is a complete nose gear steering failure, we have no steering
(30) controller:	Roger that, copy that, standby I will help you

In turn (27), the pilot states the condition of the aircraft, and in turn (28), the controller acknowledges that it needs to be towed to the gate. The pilot reiterates the condition in turn (29).

<T=7.57>
(31) controller:	Cathay 416, Incheon Ground
(32) pilot:	Incheon Ground, Cathay 416
(33) controller:	We are now coordinating the towing truck and do you need anything else to help you?
(34) pilot:	er...negative er...we don't see the tug at the time but yeah...well, your towing is in good condition just that the nose gear steering is inoperative
(35) controller:	Roger that
(36) pilot:	Ground, Cathay 416
(37) controller:	Cathay 416, Ground, go ahead
(38) pilot:	Roger, er...we had a hydraulic failure on final approach. er...there may be some runway contamination with the hydraulic fluid. er...once we've vacated the runway with the tug, er...you may want to carry out an inspection on it
(39) controller:	Roger that, we will check the runway
(40) pilot:	Thank you

In turn (33), the controller asks the pilot if anything else is needed besides a tow truck. The pilot responds *negative* and confirms that the aircraft is ready for towing in turn (34). In turn (38), the pilot informs the controller that runway 33 Right requires inspection due to hydraulic fluid leakage from a system failure, which could pose a fire risk. In subsequent turns, the pilot requests fire services.

<T=8.46>
(41) pilot:	Ground, Cathay 416
(42) controller:	Yes, go ahead
(43) pilot:	Roger, can you ask for the er...fire trucks to er...come out and just

	follow us into the bay please, due to that hydraulic fluid
(44) controller:	Roger that, fire truck copy that, I will do that
(45) pilot:	Confirming we have no situation but we would like them to just follow us in onto the bay due to er, we have a hot brake but no problem
(46) controller:	Roger that, I copy
(47) pilot:	Thank you

The pilot contacts the controller again to request a fire truck. Due to hydraulic system failure, the brakes have overheated, posing a fire risk. In turn (45), the pilot states that although there is no fire, they want the fire truck to follow the aircraft as a precaution. In subsequent turns, the pilot asks about the wait time for the tow truck and reiterates the request for the fire truck stay close to the aircraft.

<T=9.14>	
(48) pilot:	Ground, Cathay 416, is there, er, any indication of how long the tug will be?
(49) controller:	Cathay 415, expect 5 minutes, er … standby. I'll call you
(50) pilot:	Roger
(51) controller:	Cathay 416, Incheon Ground
(52) pilot:	Incheon Ground, Cathay 416, go ahead
(53) controller:	Ye, towing truck and fire truck is almost ready and it will take just a couple of minutes … and just standby
(54) pilot:	Okay, we see the fire trucks ### on the right, and er … when they do come, er … we ### that they should follow us into the bay under tow
(55) controller:	Roger
(56) pilot:	Incheon Ground, Cathay 416

In turn (48), the pilot asks how long they must wait for the tow truck, and this is answered in the following turn. In turn (53), the controller informs the pilot that the tow truck and fire truck will arrive soon. The pilot then reiterates his request for the fire truck to follow the aircraft until it reaches the gate. At this point, a third controller replaces the second, despite no indication that this second controller had difficulty understanding the pilot. During the focus group workshop with the controller informants, it was noted that the third controller had studied in the United Kingdom and was therefore expected to understand the pilot better.

4.2.3 Part Three with the Third Controller

Communication in Part Three primarily concerns fire engine services, taxiways, and crossing the runway while the aircraft is being towed. In subsequent turns, the pilot informs the controller that the aircraft is connected to the tow truck and requests a fire engineer to inspect the aircraft.

```
<T=10.18>
(57) pilot:         Incheon Ground?
(58) controller:    Roger, Cathay 416, go ahead
(59) pilot:         Cathay 416, be advised we are
                    connecting to the ground personnel
                    and the er, ground tug now
(60) controller:    Ye, we will see, we see it now

(61) pilot:         er, Ground, Cathay 416, 416, can you
                    advise we would like the er, fire
                    engines to er, come back to the
                    aircraft and inspect the aircraft
                    with the engineer?
(62) controller:    Yes, the er, the engineer is, has just
                    arrived with the towing car, so
                    standby
(63) pilot:         Affirmative, can you please get the fire
                    engines over to the aircraft, please?
```

In turn (59), the pilot informs the controller that the aircraft is connected to the tow truck. In turn (61), the pilot requests a fire personnel inspection of the aircraft. However, in turn (62), the controller appears not to understand the request and refers to the tow truck engineer instead. The pilot repeats the request in turn (63), and the request for a fire truck continues in subsequent turns.

```
<T=11.17>
(64) pilot:         Fire services to the aircraft
(65) controller:    You, you mean you want the fire, fire
                    rescue car beside you?
(66) pilot:         That's affirmative. We just had a
                    report of some er ... odour in the
                    aircraft
(67) controller:    Okay, roger
```

In turn (64), the pilot requests the fire truck again, but the controller interprets this as a new request and confirms it in turn (65). The pilot reiterates the request, explaining that there is a report of an odour in the aircraft. In subsequent turns, the pilot asks if he can speak directly with the fire personnel.

```
<T=11.39>
(68) pilot:         Incheon Ground, Cathay 416, can we
                    communicate directly with the fire
                    personnel on this frequency?
```

(69) controller:	The fire personnel is coming to you, so standby
(70) pilot:	Can we communicate directly with the fire services?
(71) controller:	Okay, standby
(72) controller:	Cathay 416, what exactly would you, would you like to ask the fire personnel? You can contact to us
(73) pilot:	Ground, Cathay 416, er, no problem, just, er, if they come, go to the rear of the aircraft and follow us in, rear of the airplane and follow us in
(74) controller:	Okay, rear of the aircraft and follow you, okay, copy
(75) pilot:	Thank you

In response to the pilot's questions in turns (68) and (70), the controller initially does not provide appropriate answers. When asked if the pilot can speak directly with the fire personnel, she first responds that they are on their way and later gives a positive response in turn (71). After agreeing to the pilot's request for direct communication, the controller asks in turn (72) what the pilot wants the fire personnel to do. In turn (73), the pilot replies that he wants them to inspect the rear of the aircraft and follow closely.

In subsequent turns, the controller verifies whether there is an actual odour report on the aircraft. Communication then continues regarding the taxiways the aircraft will use and runway crossing clearance en route to the assigned gate.

<T=12.37>	
(76) controller:	Cathay 416, do you er...te...did someone report of strange er...smell or smoke in the airplane?
(77) pilot:	Cathay 416, negative, it's precautionary only, precautionary only
(78) controller:	Okay
(79) pilot:	Thank you
(80) controller:	Cathay 416, do you have the contact with the towing personnel?
(81) pilot:	Cathay 416, we have contact with the towing personnel and tow equipment is connected and er...looks like now we are ready to do taxi and requesting taxi to er...to bay 46 and clearance to cross the parallel runway 33 Left
(82) controller:	Cathay 416, expect your taxiway Charlie 4, Charlie then Kilo and you will cross 33 Left via Kilo

(83) pilot: Okay, I think we are going to have to er, take to clear Charlie 5, er... so we will take that as Charlie 5 and Kilo and er... we will hold short of 33 Left
(84) controller: Cathay 416, you mean you cannot vacate runway via Charlie 4?
(85) pilot: er... No, we are too far. We passed the ending point. (1.2) Negative
(86) controller: Okay, we will tell the towing personnel to move you to Charlie 5, so er... if you need anything please talk to the towing personnel
(87) pilot: Roger, we will do and just confirm we are going Charlie 5, Kilo and hold short of 33 Left
(88) controller: That's affirmative
(89) pilot: Okay, er... we'll call you holding short of 33 Left, Cathay 416
(90) controller: Cathay 416, advise you, you don't need the er... taxi instruction with this radio frequency. We will talk to the towing personnel directly, so, don't worry
(91) pilot: Okay, er, we take that, thank you
(92) pilot: And Seoul, Cathay 416, do you want us to remain on this frequency?
(93) controller: That's affirmative
(94) pilot: Roger, will do
(95) pilot: Ground, Cathay 416, it appears that the truck drivers are taking us er, further up to er, taxiway Kilo, is that confirmed?
(96) controller: Standby, we are checking

The presence of an odour report is checked in turns (76) through (79), and towing is verified in turns (80) and (81). In turn (81), the pilot requests information on the taxiways to be used and runway clearance. In turn (82), the controller lists the taxiways up to the runway point. Between turns (83) and (86), one taxiway is changed because the aircraft has already passed it, and this change is confirmed between turns (87) and (89). In turn (90), the controller states that direct communication with the pilot is unnecessary, as she will communicate directly with the tow truck personnel. However, communication continues because the aircraft is being directed differently than instructed. The pilot maintains communication with the controller to stay informed about all taxiways and runway crossing clearance. After turn (96), there is a 57-second of no communication.

```
<T=16.39>
(97) controller:    Cathay 416, (1.2) Cathay 416, we told
                    the towing personnel to move you
                    to the Kilo
(98) pilot:         Roger, we copy that we are going to
                    Kilo and er ... please confirm with
                    us when we are cleared to cross 33
                    Left. We would like to be advised all
(99) controller:    Okay
(100) pilot:        Thank you
```

While the aircraft is being towed, the pilot requests updates on taxiways and runway crossing clearance in turn (98), and the controller agrees to provide them in turn (99).

In subsequent turns, the pilot continues to confirm runway crossing clearance. Meanwhile, the assigned gate number changes, requiring adjustments to the taxiways. Miscommunication between the controller and the Korean tow truck personnel prolongs communication between the pilot and controller.

```
<T=17.03>
(101) controller:   Cathay 416, do you see the red lights?
(102) pilot:        Affirmative
(103) controller:   You will be stopped before that
(104) pilot:        Roger, holding short of 33 Left

(105) controller:   Cathay 416, is, are your engines all
                    shut down?
(106) pilot:        Affirmative
(107) controller:   Roger

(108) pilot:        And, just for the confirmation with
                    Cathay 416, confirm cleared to
                    cross 33 Left
(109) controller:   That's affirmative
(110) pilot:        Thank you, Cathay 416

(111) controller:   Cathay 416, your gate number has been
                    changed to number 43 and you will be
                    taxied via Alpha then Alpha 8
(112) pilot:        Alpha and Alpha 8 to bay 43 now, thank
                    you, Cathay 416

(113) pilot:        Ground, Cathay 416, it appears we are
                    now, er, being directed on Bravo,
                    be advised

(114) pilot:        Ground, Cathay 416
(115) controller:   Cathay 416, I'm sorry. We have er ...
                    a communication problem with the
                    towing personnel. You will be taxied
                    via Alpha 14 then Alpha
```

(116) pilot:	Alpha 14 and Alpha, okay, Cathay 416
(117) pilot:	And, from Cathay 416, it looks like er... your plan has been changed to Alpha 15 and then Bravo
(118) controller:	er, what direction are you heading now?
(119) pilot:	er, we, I'm just commenting ((I want to know)) what the FOLLOW ME[6] vehicle is doing. He changed the direction and he is now er... directing on Alpha 15 and Bravo
(120) pilot:	We are on Alpha 15 now
(121) controller:	Cathay 416, contact ramp 121 decimal 65
(122) pilot:	121 decimal 65 for ramp, Cathay 416, thank you

In turn (108), the pilot confirms runway crossing clearance. In turn (111), the gate number changes, prompting adjustments to the taxiways. Due to miscommunication between the tower and two truck personnel, a different taxiway is assigned in turn (115). In subsequent turns, the *Follow Me* car takes a different route, which the pilot notes in turn (119). The situation is quickly resolved, and communication concludes with the pilot receiving the ramp contact frequency in turns (121) and (122).

4.3 Domain Specialists' Evaluations

As noted in Section 4.1.3, the two main superordinate themes relevant to the performance of the Australian pilot and the three Korean controllers are DOMAIN ASPECTS and LANGUAGE ASPECTS. Each subordinate theme is presented here, although not in equal details. The level of detail reflects the amount of time the informants devoted to each theme; for example, the informants were particularly enthusiastic in sharing their experiences and anecdotes when topics such as intelligibility and accent variation were discussed. The Australian pilot, who engaged in radiotelephony communication, was evaluated by the informants as notably lacking 'professional knowledge' and 'experience' in handling the situation, as highlighted under DOMAIN ASPECTS. With LANGUAGE ASPECTS, his failure to 'accommodate' to his L2+ interlocutors, particularly in terms of 'vocabulary' and 'speech rate', was also significant. Furthermore, his 'accent' and 'speech rate' prompted discussion on 'intelligibility' in radiotelephony communication and related workplace challenges.

---

[6] Follow Me is a vehicle with a large 'FOLLOW ME' sign on it. When an aircraft arrives at the airport for the first time, the vehicle guides it to the gate via taxiways.

Concerning the first Korean controller, the informants noted his limited 'comprehension' of the pilot's plain English and insufficient 'English proficiency' under LANGUAGE ASPECTS, as well as his habitual use of *roger* without understanding the messages, which was coded as 'professional competence' under DOMAIN ASPECTS. In contrast, the second and third Korean controllers were frequently recognised for their strong 'English proficiency', while their lack or absence of 'professional knowledge' was evaluated negatively. In presenting the informants' comments, single quotation marks are used when quoting. In block quotations, capital letters denote emphatic stress by the informants, while square brackets are used for my own comments.

4.3.1 Domain Aspects

The most prominent theme was the 'professional knowledge' of the Australian pilot and the two Korean controllers in Parts Two and Three of the discourse, which was harshly evaluated due to their limited understanding of how to handle this abnormal situation. Typically, when an aircraft loses steering and requires towing, communication occurs between a controller and a tow truck driver, eliminating the need for pilot-controller interaction. However, in this case, the pilot requested updates on every step, prompting the controller to provide detailed responses after each request. Although the two controllers complied actively – as noted by the informants with slight sarcasm – this resulted in unnecessarily prolonged exchanges characterised by numerous confirmations and clarifications. Controller Informant 2 questioned who was in charge during the incident and criticised the responsible party for allowing inefficient and extended communication. He stated:

> All they needed to do was TOW the aircraft. The communication between the pilot and controller was unnecessary. Consider what the controller was saying: *You'll be going this way and that way, blah, blah, blah*, and so on. Since the aircraft had lost its ability to taxi, there was no need to communicate with the pilot. All communication between the pilot and the controller was pointless because the aircraft was being towed by the TOW TRUCK! The aircraft couldn't taxi on its own, so it was the controllers who needed to communicate with the tow truck driver. If we say *stop*, then it stops; if we say *go*, it goes. This controller kept telling the pilot what was happening, where the aircraft would be going, and what it would be passing through. What did they think they were doing? Were they practising English by listening and repeating? That was useless. The controller asked if the engines were all shut down—how on earth could we tow the aircraft with its engines on?

Pilot Informant 1 stated that, in an abnormal situation, a pilot should first contact their company to discuss the issue and request further assistance. The informant noted that the Australian pilot should have initially contacted Cathay Pacific for cooperation. All three pilot informants commented on the pilot's lack of 'professional knowledge' and 'experience' in managing this type of situation. Two pilot informants suggested that the cockpit crew must have been aware of the hydraulic failure earlier, as detecting it at this stage of flight was unlikely; thus, transmitting this information after initiating landing was inappropriate.

Regarding the first controller, all informants remarked that his use of *roger* without fully understanding the previous message, was the most significant fault in his performance. Controller Informant 1 criticised this behaviour, stating that perfect accuracy is vital in air traffic control and that 'uncertainty in radiotelephony is unforgivable'. Similarly, Pilot Informant 2 put it:

> The most dangerous aspect here is the controller's use of *roger* at the end of each contact [referring to turns 9, 13, and 20]. *Roger* means 'I understand your previous message', but he just assumed that it was not significant and required no special attention.

Some informants noted that the habitual use of *roger* by certain controllers constitutes poor practice, as it implies understanding of transmitted messages. Consequently, pilots may assume the message has been understood, which can ultimately lead to miscommunication. Regarding the first controller, although the process was not smooth, his eventual understanding of the situation and instruction for the next aircraft to go around was positively evaluated ('professional competence').

Regarding the change of controllers, particularly the transition from the second to the third, two pilot informants noted that this was an ill-advised decision, as changing controllers mid-communication hindered the maintenance of consistent situational awareness, especially given that the second controller managed the situation effectively. This issue was coded as 'other' within DOMAIN ASPECTS, as it pertains more to managerial decisions within the air traffic unit. The third controller's 'professional competence' was negatively evaluated; as Pilot Informant 3 remarked, she actively responded to the pilot's requests 'without knowing what she was doing'.

4.3.2 Language Aspects

Plain English is expected to be used in this abnormal situation. As observed, communication between the Australian pilot and the second and third controllers on a separate frequency was conducted in colloquial English, except for standard phraseology such as *roger, affirmative,* and call signs. This allows the reader to follow the transmissions without difficulty, although background knowledge is necessary to understand the context.

The most commented-on features were 'vocabulary' and 'comprehension', followed by the first Korean controller's insufficient 'English proficiency' and the Australian pilot's excessively fast 'speech rate'. The pilot's speech was measured at approximately 255 words per minute, 2.5 times faster than the recommended 100 words per minute. Although this aspect could be coded under DOMAIN ASPECTS, as it aligns with ICAO's radiotelephony communication guidelines (ICAO, 2016), the informants acknowledged that faster communication is sometimes unavoidable in busy traffic. Therefore, it was coded under LANGUAGE ASPECTS. The informants criticised the pilot's rapid 'speech rate' in this instance as inconsiderate towards his L2+ controllers, coded as 'non-accommodation', particularly during an abnormal situation that requires extra workload, especially since the communication occurred on a separate frequency. This was identified as a contributing factor to repeated and prolonged turns.

Regarding 'vocabulary', the Australian pilot's use of the word *tug* was discussed. The pilot used *tug* both as a noun and a verb in the episode. Of the three controller informants, only one was familiar with the term, while all pilot informants recognised it. Pilot Informant 2 noted that *tow truck* is more commonly used and that understanding *tug* as a verb was challenging, even in context. He stated:

> I knew the meaning of the word *tug* but I don't think I could have understood it if I had heard it as the pilot said, [tʌg] [tʌg]. I understand the word because I'm looking at the transcript. We're more familiar with *towing car* ... This pilot never tried to use the terms *tug car* or *tug vehicle* to clarify, but instead used *tug* as a verb repeatedly: *tug, tug* to where, *tug,* and *tug.*

The Australian pilot's use of the words *odour, rear,* and *fire engine* were also discussed. The controller informants suggested that *smell* would have been easier to understand, and Pilot Informant 2 recommended using *smell* instead of *odour* and *behind* instead of *rear* in this context. However, Pilot Informant 3 argued that the pilot's word choices were not difficult to understand and criticised those unprepared for English vocabulary use in abnormal or emergency situations. He said:

> A word like *odour* is basic. It would be odd if someone didn't understand it ... Anyway, there are only three words that could be used in this situation: *smell, odour,* or *scent.* To me, it doesn't sound proper to use *smell* here, and *odour* is often used. It's the same when we make an in-flight announcement to passengers about this. There are only three options, so it isn't too much to ask.

The controller informant group was unaware that *fire engine* is synonymous with *fire truck*. Despite its appearance in the transcript, considerable time was spent trying to understand its meaning in context. Pilot Informant 1 later confirmed the usage.

The theme 'comprehension' was the next most commented-on aspect. All informants agreed that the first controller did not understand the pilot's message in plain English, and some informants also noted the controller's inadequate 'English proficiency'. Two controller informants suggested possible distractions, such as the controller's attention being diverted to the next aircraft, which may have impaired his understanding. When asked whether the first controller's English proficiency was insufficient, Pilot Informant 3 responded 'not necessarily, as he eventually understood the situation and instructed the following aircraft to go around', emphasising the controller's eventual recognition and response. However, Pilot Informant 2 considered the controller's English proficiency problematic, despite the pilot's communicative flaw of speaking too rapidly when delivering the critical message and suggested that a lack of knowledge about such situations may also have contributed. He said:

> Firstly, in turn (8), the controller did not understand the message when the pilot initially stated that the aircraft would be stopping on the runway, prompting the pilot to repeat the message in turn (10). Despite this, the controller, unaware of the issue with the aircraft, instructed the pilot to vacate the runway. The pilot responded with *negative, negative* to the instruction, but the controller insisted on vacating the runway without delay. The controller did not understand the pilot at all . . . The controller's lack of understanding was partly due to insufficient knowledge of flight operations or aircraft systems and partly due to inadequate English proficiency.

The theme of 'intelligibility' was highlighted, as the informants struggled to understand and transcribe the Australian pilot's turns, which were further complicated by his excessively fast speech. The informants generalised about the relatively challenging L1-influenced English accents of many L2+ pilots and controllers from countries such as China, Japan, Korea, Russia, South America, and Vietnam. Pilots on a radio frequency can hear all transmissions made on that frequency. When asked if he often heard the request *say again* over Incheon airspace, Pilot Informant 3 responded as follows:

> Yes, I frequently hear requests to *say again* in Korean airspace, and the same occurs in Japanese airspace. American and British pilots, in particular, have trouble understanding controllers in Japanese airspace due to their English pronunciation. It's easy for us Koreans but difficult for them. EVERYONE has trouble in China, and EVERYONE has difficulty understanding in Arab regions.

He continued by providing specific examples including a Korean controller with a strong Korean-influenced accent – some varieties of Korean are recognised as strong or more difficult to understand compared with the so-called Seoul variety – and a Japanese controller communicating in standard phraseology with English L1 pilots. He mimicked these accents, in a rather exaggerated manner, demonstrating features such as consonant approximation, consonant and vowel epenthesis, and incorrect word stress. He noted that these features may cause difficulty for interlocutors who have not been exposed to them and are therefore unfamiliar with such patterns. The stressed syllables are underlined in the following quote:

> It IS problematic. Let me give you an example. While a Korean controller was communicating with an American jet for departure at Jeju [an island located in southern Korea], she said *cleared for take-off*, and the jet took off. The controller then instructed the pilot *maintain runway hedi:ɪŋŋ, klaimb ænd meintei:nn fo sauzənd:ɯ faivɯ hʌndred:ɯ* [maintain runway heading, climb and maintain 4 thousand and 5 hundred]. How on earth could the pilot possibly understand that? No way! She must have tried hard to make it work. She THOUGHT she spoke clearly and loudly, but it just didn't work. WE Koreans can understand it, but there's no way for others [non-Koreas] to do so. The US Air Force in Korea might understand it because they know how Koreans pronounce English. The Korean controller must have wondered *how could he not understand my slow and enunciated clear pronunciation?* when she was asked to repeat it multiple times. And what about the Japanese? They say *tə:rn lefto hedi:ŋgu zeroh nainer zeroh klaimu ænd meintein* [turn left heading zero nine zero, climb and maintain].

Pilot Informant 3 emphasised the challenge of managing L1-influenced pronunciations ('local accents') in the international and multilingual radiotelephony context. Notably, within the international aviation community – particularly in Korea – there is a culture of studying the pronunciation and accent features of the destination country prior to flying. He said:

> When it comes to pronunciation, it's not just about us; it's the same all over the world. What I'm saying is that while it's important to make an effort to change one's pronunciation if many others find it hard to understand, it is more important to STUDY the unique features of pronunciations before flying into other countries by listening to recorded tapes. That's what professionals do!

He added that this practice is especially important for pilots flying to a country for the first time. He noted that many pilots in Korea follow this practice, and most captains have a better ability to understand various accents, as it typically takes about ten years or more for an ab initio pilot to become a captain. While emphasising this practice as a professional standard, his anecdotal experience flying over São Paulo reveals the challenges caused by unfamiliarity with the local accent in practice. He described:

> Still, South America remains a region where I lack confidence. I've only flown there a few times, and those experiences have been challenging. Once, while flying over São Paulo, a controller said something I couldn't understand, even after *say again* three times. In the end, a pilot of an American aircraft stepped in said *There is a balloon, a hot air balloon ascending, so watch out for it* . . . [the author asked if that kind of interruption was acceptable, and he replied] The pilot stepped in because I was clearly struggling.

He further noted that captains, as experienced professionals, rigorously adhere to the practice of preparing for various accents, whereas some first officers do not, for various reasons.

All informants criticised the pilot's excessively fast 'speech rate' throughout the transmissions, but Pilot Informant 2 specifically mentioned that, in Part One, the pilot delivered the critical message that the aircraft would stop on the runway in a monotonous and routine-sounding manner, which failed to capture the controller's attention in radiotelephony. He stated:

> If I were the pilot, I would slow down the rate of speech when conveying the message. I would clearly and slowly say, *Be advised, we will be stopping on the runway* [speaking very slowly] or *Be advised, we will remain on the runway after landing* [speaking slowly], rather than just add *we'll be stopping on the runway* in his clearance readback. I don't think changing tone would help, as it could increase stress in a tense situation and affect situational awareness. However, speaking slowly would be beneficial.

During the workshop sessions, I was surprised to learn that this type of situation is not classified as either an urgency or an emergency. Therefore, the Australian pilot was not expected to declare a state of urgency. No message marker signals such situations, even though follow-up measures or assistance might be needed. This prompted a discussion on the 'inadequacy of existing standard phraseology and radiotelephony conventions'. The informants highlighted the lack of signal words to indicate abnormal situations. In standard phraseology, two distress calls are used: *mayday* for emergencies and *pan pan* for urgency (ICAO, 2016). Since no specific phraseology exists for abnormal situations, pilots must rely on their ability to use plain English. Two controller informants argued that this episode should have been declared an emergency because the aircraft lost steering completely and stopped on the runway, disrupting air traffic flow. However, all agreed that declaring emergencies depends on a pilot's judgement, and all pilot informants stated this situation could not be classified as an emergency.

Pilot Informant 3 expressed regret over the absence of radiotelephony conventions for alerting controllers in such situations. Regarding this issue, Pilot Informant 1 suggested implementing a repeat obligation for the controller. He commented:

> In fact, only pilots are currently obligated to repeat messages. However, making it compulsory for controllers to repeat an important message could be beneficial. For example, if a pilot says *I'll remain on the runway after landing* along with a signalling word for repetition, the controller will then repeat, *You'll remain on the runway after landing*. Of course, there should be a standardised word or phrase for this purpose. In such cases, extra effort should be made to speak slowly and clearly.

Lastly, as mentioned earlier, all informants recognised the good 'English proficiency' of the second and third controllers in a rather cynical manner. Their 'active' and 'too friendly' responses to the Australian pilot, as noted by the informants, were in fact unnecessary and were further compounded by their lack of knowledge.

4.3.3 Other

The themes 'ICAO English proficiency requirements' and 'review of transcript and context' were categorised under OTHER, with the former briefly presented in this section. Pilot Informant 2 criticised the ICAO requirements, stating that English proficiency is irrelevant or even dangerous when attempting to communicate detailed information during abnormal situations. Referring to a similar experience with hydraulic failure but in an urgent situation, he stated:

> Even when a controller asks us something, we don't even respond right away. Everyone's lives are at risk. We in the cockpit might look calm, but we're actually busy dealing with our own urgent tasks to keep the aircraft safe. Trying to speak good English in that situation? That could even jeopardise safety. We don't bother. Once we've handled what we need to, then we can respond or communicate.

Pilot Informant 3 emphasised that this episode highlights an issue of efficiency rather than a safety concern in communication. He noted that while a basic level of English proficiency is necessary for aviation personnel to ensure service quality, testing the use of standard phraseology is more important than assessing English proficiency. He commented that noncompliance with standard phraseology is not only a problem among English L1 aviation personnel. He stated 'In reality, a team leader controller, who is themself a non-native speaker with twenty years of experience, does not use standard phraseology'.

5 Discussion and Recommendations

This study aimed to investigate various aspects affecting pilot-controller radiotelephony communication in the context of aviation ELF by examining naturally occurring discourse and insights from domain specialists, to interpret these within the community of practice framework, and to critique the ICAO English proficiency testing policy from this perspective. The three previously posed research questions are addressed here, with relevant recommendations offered for each. Some aspects overlap across the research questions; these are reiterated more concise when repeated, as they offer different implications from distinct perspectives.

5.1 Research Question 1: What Aviation Specialists Value

The first research question is *what language-specific and domain-specific aspects emerge from domain specialists' evaluations of peers' performance in naturally occurring situations?* The domain- and language-specific aspects reported in Section 4 are discussed in relation to four key themes: the interplay between domain knowledge and language use; accommodation and lack thereof; managing various accents; and the need for greater standardisation in radiotelephony communication.

5.1.1 The Interplay between Domain Knowledge and Language Use

In the episode involving a tow request after an aircraft hydraulic failure, the informants generally agreed that the first Korean controller had difficulty understanding the Australian pilot's repeated messages. Some also noted that the pilot's failure to signal the abnormal situation contributed to this non-understanding or misunderstanding. While several informants attributed the issue primarily to the controller's inadequate English proficiency, one pilot also cited the controller's lack of knowledge about potential events during that flight phase. Conversely, another pilot informant praised the controller's eventual understanding and his decision to instruct the following aircraft to go around. That is, despite the initial lack of understanding in the context, the controller's domain knowledge and experience ultimately informed his professional judgment and actions.

A similar interplay was observed in evaluations of the second and third Korean controllers. While their English proficiency was commended, the informants criticised their lack of professional knowledge, which resulted in convergent accommodation towards the pilot but also lengthy and unnecessary communication. The controller informants specifically considered the entire transmission unnecessary, as standard protocol limits communication to the controller and the tow truck driver. Additionally, the informants regarded the Australian pilot's request to be involved in these communications as interference with the controllers' duties and thus professionally inappropriate, though they noted that the pilot's desire to stay informed was understandable given the stressful situation.

These findings align with those of my previous study (Kim, 2018), where a Korean controller's limited knowledge of airways, despite better English proficiency, led to prolonged and unclear communication with a Russian pilot. These observations also corroborate Knoch's (2014) validation study, which found that English L1 pilot domain specialists placed greater value on *technical knowledge*, *experience*, and *training level* than on language aspects. The episode in present study, along with others, highlights the inevitable interplay between domain knowledge and language use in professional settings (Douglas, 2000, 2023): strong English proficiency alone does not confer an advantage and may, in fact, prolong communication inefficiencies, thereby posing risks to air safety in radiotelephony contexts.

The minimal importance placed on English proficiency by the domain specialists in this study echoes Elder et al.'s (2012) findings in a healthcare setting, where experts rarely mentioned English proficiency or other language-related aspects in their evaluations. Although the threshold level remains unknown, De Andrade's (2023) study in Brazil shows that controllers with the pre-operational level 3 on the local test reported feeling confident in international radiotelephony communication, even though level 4 is the official standard. Another related issue is whether aviation safety is genuinely enhanced by removing senior pilots and controllers solely for failing to meet the minimum standard. This concern is reflected in Kim and Elder's (2015) surveys and interviews, which indicate that many Korean pilots and controllers fear such measures may increase, rather than reduce, safety risks. Furthermore, with respect to the ICAO testing policy, it is questionable whether it is possible – or even fair – to assess true competence in aviation ELF, or any other professional ELF context, when available tests focus solely on language skills. This issue is further discussed in Sections 5.2 and 5.3.

5.1.2 (Lack of) Accommodation Skills

Accommodation is a skill emphasised from early aviation ELF studies (e.g., Kim & Billington, 2018; Kim & Elder, 2009), alongside the concept of shared responsibility for the success or failure of communication among interlocutors with varying degrees of English proficiency and domain expertise. In the episode examined in this study, the Australian pilot's lack of accommodation skills was the most frequently commented-on feature, particularly regarding his rapid speech rate and word choice. While his fast speech rate was sympathised with, given the rare and stressful abnormal situation, his continued rapid speech after being assigned a separate frequency demonstrated inexperience, as noted by the informants, in handing abnormal situations and communicating with L2+ controllers. The informants also criticised his word choice (e.g., using *tug* both as a noun and a verb, *fire engine*, *odour*, and *rear*) as inconsiderate, since the pilot made no effort to modify these terms despite indications of the controllers' delayed understanding. These findings echo the American pilot's lack of consideration for a Korean controller in Kim and Elder (2009), where a fast rate of speech and verbose, colloquial English were criticised. In other words, both English L1 pilots failed to adjust their language for their controller conversational partners, or more accurately, they may not have been aware that such an adjustment would have been beneficial, as it would have improved the situation for themselves as well. These nonaccommodative aspects, evidenced by maintenance strategies (Dragojevic et al., 2016), stand in stark contrast to the findings of ELF studies in other contexts, such as Seidlhofer (2009), in which there was strong and creative update of the phrase *endangered field*, uttered by a previous interlocutor and subsequently adapted by others in later turns, and Pitzl (2009), in which understanding of a direct translation of a German idiom was achieved collaboratively within a situated business context. Similar nonaccommodation was observed in Kim's (2018) study – manifested more in communicative behaviour in this case – involving a Korean controller who, due to a lack of knowledge, fixated solely on the task he was struggling with and failed to respond to or confirm the Russian pilot's strategic efforts to ensure understanding.

Regarding the extent to which training on vocabulary is needed in international radiotelephony communication, one pilot informant's comment is revealing. He noted that a relatively small vocabulary repertoire is required for aviation, for example, describing all *smell*-related words such as *smell*, *odour*, or *scent*. With respect to accommodation skills in aviation ELF, alongside the importance of shared responsibility for communication, learning words for use and understanding in abnormal situations constitutes a way of sharing responsibility among L2+ pilots and controllers. The same applies to English L1 pilots and controllers. Specifically, recognising non-understanding in context and adjusting their language accordingly, along with slowing speech rate, are skills they can develop and prepare for. In other words, although some might anticipate the exclusion of *scent* due to its positive connotation in describing a fire situation, the ability to recognise it as a variant when introduced by interlocutors is an important aspect of competence.

The ability to recognise variants that arise in context recalls that most accommodation in L1 contexts across disciplines is unconscious and automatic, as reviewed by Gasiorek (2016). In ELF contexts, however, more conscious and strategic adjustments become necessary, requiring participants' awareness and deliberate effort due to an unshared L1 linguistic repertoire. This is supported by evidence of collaborative interaction, including understanding achieved through mutual effort, observed in ELF studies (e.g., Cogo, 2009; Gaete, 2022; Kaur, 2009; Kaur & Birlik, 2021; Seidlhofer, 2009). This highlights the importance of raising conscious awareness and attentiveness to the variation that interlocutors bring to interactions in the international radiotelephony context. As observed with the Australian pilot in this study and in previous research, some pilots and controllers either do not recognise the need for accommodation or lack the ability to do so – likely due to insufficient exposure to international contexts or limited experience. Another possible reason for this lack of awareness is that, as implied by the ICAO testing policy with 'native speakers' exemption, it may be assumed that the responsibility lies solely with less proficient L2+ users to 'life their game', as noted by Kim and Elder (2009). If this is the case, it would in effect increase the potential risks associated with communication issues in real-life radiotelephony.

Not all convergence strategies are valued by the informants. The accepting and supportive responses of the second and third Korean controllers to the Australian pilot's request for updates, along with their use of colloquial English to accommodate the pilot, can be considered convergence, as briefly mentioned previously; however, these actions were harshly criticised by the informants. In this case, convergent accommodation occurred in violation of protocol, resulting in severe inefficiency. An Australia pilot informant's note in Kim and Friginal (2026) provides insight into this issue. He stated that some L2+ controllers adhere strictly to standard phraseology in response, serving as a reminder for pilots to use it when they employ plain or colloquial English. This adherence – a maintenance strategy – acts as a cautionary measure to ensure safe and efficient radiotelephony communication. Although this maintenance strategy is a non-accommodative feature, it can function as a desirable safeguard in radiotelephony communication. Overall, all accommodation strategies, whether convergence, maintenance, or even divergence, can be strategically adopted when found to be useful for more effective radiotelephony communication.

5.1.3 Dealing with a Variety of English-speaking Accents

As mentioned earlier, considerable time was spent transcribing the Australian pilot's turns verbatim in collaboration with the controller informants, particularly due to the pilot's rapid speech. In other ELF communication settings, accents are often discussed in terms of users' preferences or aspirations towards dominant varieties, such as American and British, or attitudes, rather than as challenges to comprehension (e.g., Galloway & Rose, 2015; Jenkins, 2007). However, accents can pose significant challenges in real-world, voice-only radiotelephony communication under noisy conditions, potentially jeopardising both efficiency and safety. Indeed, the difficulty of managing a variety of accents is consistently identified as a core but challenging aspect of radiotelephony communication (e.g., Kim, 2018; Kim & Billington, 2018; Kim & Elder, 2015; Tiewtrakul & Fletcher, 2010). It is important to note that this challenge is not limited to L2+ speakers but also affects English L1 pilots and controllers (Kim & Friginal, 2026; Knoch, 2014).

One pilot informant in this study commented that most captains are better at dealing with various accents than first officers, due to their more extensive exposure and acquired skills developed over a longer career trajectory. His conjecture that US Air Force pilots residing in Korea should be able to understand Korean-influenced English accents can be understood in a similar vein: familiarity with accents is crucial. A contrasting but related experience is his account of struggling when flying to the South American region, where he had rarely flown before. This anecdote underscores the importance of familiarity through exposure in practice (discussed further in Section 5.2). These observations align with findings from studies by Tauroza and Luk (1997) in the Hong Kong context and Smith and Nelson (2020) in the American context, both of which emphasise the role of familiarity, especially through long-term exposure.

The practice of Korean pilots listening to various accents prior to their first flights offers valuable insight. This is an example of what individuals do in real-life practice, yet researchers have been slow to offer practical recommendations. More formally shared repertoires of audio recordings, organised internationally (e.g., through ICAO), would benefit the entire pilot and controller populations. Additionally, one informant's observation that some Korean controllers' English pronunciation features pose challenges for non-Koreans – revealed through his mimicry of consonant approximation, consonant epenthesis, and incorrect word stress – provides further insight. As recommended by Kim and Billington (2018), increased awareness of which L1-influenced features are most likely to cause comprehension difficulties for others, along with the ability to accommodate accordingly, as also argued by Jenkins (2000, 2007), would greatly benefit the international aviation context. Furthermore, in light of growing research on ELF, more studies are needed on phonological features influenced by various L1 backgrounds that affect intelligibility, moving beyond comparisons in terms of 'standard' or 'native' English pronunciations and 'non-native' pronunciations.

5.1.4 More Standardisation for Radiotelephony Communication

Although the theme 'inadequacy of existing standard phraseology and radiotelephony conventions' under LANGUAGE ASPECTS was only briefly mentioned in Section 4 – since it was not directly relevant to the performance of the pilot and the three controllers in the recording – it nonetheless presents an important point of discussion with significant implications. As previously noted, there is currently no standardised message marker to signal the type of abnormal situation, a feature that would have greatly improved the transmission in Part One. In the absence of such markers, pilots must rely on plain English and other linguistic strategies, which are not always effective. The introduction of an initial message marker (e.g., *attention attention*) to draw a controller's attention to abnormal stations, as well as a marker (e.g., *request rephrase*) to explicitly signal a request for clarification, would serve as a reminder of both the context and the standard procedure. This could reduce the reliance on plain English, which varies among users and is therefore unpredictable. Additionally, in this context, an obligatory repeat by controllers could help prevent non-understanding or misunderstanding of critical messages, as suggested by one pilot informant in this study. Under current conventions, such obligatory repeats (i.e., readback) are only required of pilots to confirm instructions received from controllers. The addition of a message marker combined with a repeat convention for critical messages would be a simple and cost-effective measure that could substantially improve message delivery and confirmation.

This inadequacy of existing standard phraseology and radiotelephony conventions was also observed in the episode described by Kim and Billington (2018), where a controller used the phrase *taxi forward* for better traffic flow to instruct a pilot to move slightly so that the aircraft behind could pass. While emergency situations are inherently unpredictable, many commonly occurring abnormal situations could benefit greatly from an extension of current standard phraseology and improved conventions. Regarding this issue, I have made similar arguments (Kim, 2024), as have other scholars (Drayton & Coxhead, 2023; Jones, 2003; Morrow et al., 1994). These responsibilities remain with ICAO so that it can make genuine contributions to air safety.

5.2 Research Question 2: Understanding Practice in Communities of Practice

The second research question addresses *how do domain specialists' values inform the understanding of performance in radiotelephony within the framework of communities of practice?* The findings of this study, as well as relevant previous research, are discussed within the framework of communities of practice described in Section 2.

As described in Section 2, pilots and controllers engaged in international radiotelephony communication hold multiple memberships across several communities of practice. The managerial decision to replace the controllers in the episode examined in this study – particularly the replacement of the second controller with the third, not based on experience or expertise but on the latter's background of having studied in the United Kingdom – along with the two controllers' 'too friendly' responses to the Australian pilot, which compromised protocol, reveals a perceived obligation within the Korean controller community to accommodate English L1 pilots, especially under current ICAO policy. This sense of obligation suggests that it is preferable, or at least more favourably perceived, to handle requests in accordance with the contextual norms of that community.

Additionally, the careless use of terms such as *roger*, *affirmative*, and *wilco* without a true understanding of interlocutors' messages, as well as a reluctance to acknowledge non-understanding or misunderstanding, are common within these communities of practice. There also appears to be a misconception – reinforced by ICAO – that those proficient in English do not need to comply with standard phraseology because they can use plain or natural English; as one informant lamented, even an experienced team leader does not adhere to standard phraseology. These factors suggest that acknowledging misunderstanding – and thus admitting a lack of proficiency in English – may be stigmatised, rather than recognised as a proactive, safety-conscious professional act, and that such undesirable practices are wrongly perceived as competent within these communities of practice. These aspects appear to be linked to discourse within the communities and Korean society, thereby necessitating a constructionist approach that focusses on latent aspects (Braun & Clarke, 2006), as mentioned earlier in Section 4.

Lave (2019) and Lave and Wenger (1991) underline that when examining a community of practice and apprenticeship within it, historical, social, and political aspects need to be considered. As English has long served as a lingua franca in aviation since its onset in many countries, it is difficult to separate these aspects from the global role of the English language. Although English occupies an unprecedented and powerful role as a global lingua franca, characterised by diverse variations among its users (Galloway & Rose, 2015), many learners and users aspire to achieve or perform 'native' or 'native-like' proficiency, along with the associated benefits, by conforming to norms derived from dominant varieties such as American and British English in real-world contexts (e.g., Holliday, 2009; Piller, 2002). Korea, where English functions as a foreign language, is no exception; English occupies a hegemonic position within this English-frenzied society, and self-deprecation concerning perceived English incompetence is deeply ingrained as an ideological construct, making proficiency in English symbolic capital while simultaneously positioning Koreans as 'illegitimate' English speakers subordinate to 'native speakers' (Park, 2009). Similar dynamics, influenced to varying degrees by historical and cultural backgrounds, may be observed in other L2+ countries, including within their aviation communities of practice.

Within these ideological forces, the expertise assigned to 'native speakers' and the deficiency imposed on 'non-native speakers' (Holliday, 2018; Piller & Bodis 2022) in radiotelephony communication, as mentioned in the introduction, reinforce the expectation that L2+ pilots and controllers should (be able to) accommodate English L1 counterparts when requests arise, as well as a desire to demonstrate such proficiency. It also fosters sympathy for English L1 pilots' desire to be informed at every step – even when this conflicts with established protocol, as illustrated by the episode in this study. Thus, tension exists between expectations when communicating with English L1 pilots and established practices for managing such situations, as was evident when the informants acted as evaluators of their peers' performance.

All aviation communities of practice are likely shaped by what members learn through their apprenticeship within their local communities and societies, including knowledge, skills, beliefs, and values. While overgeneralising about certain communities is undesirable and should not affect individual interaction, especially in the context of intercultural communication (Kim & Penry Williams, 2021), common perceptions about particular communities can, to some extent, be understood within this framework. For example, as noted by Kim and Elder (2009) and Kim and Friginal (2026), the American aviation community is well known for its members' non-observance of radiotelephony conventions. The Korean and Australian informants in these studies also shared numerous anecdotes, based on their experience, concerning specific pronunciation patterns within particular L1 aviation communities and customary practices.

While it would be ideal for pilots and controllers to possess the expertise to manage as many variations as possible, significant challenges remain in real-world settings. Although all informants in this study had extensive experience, two controllers reported being unfamiliar with the word *tug*, used as both a noun and a verb by the Australian pilot throughout the transmissions. Additionally, one pilot noted that, although he knew the word, he would not have understood it when used in that particular rapidly uttered context. Similarly, despite preparing for a flight to an unfamiliar region by listening to an audio recording, another pilot informant – who characterised himself as competent in managing various accents encountered while flying in different regions – described difficulties he experienced over São Paulo in understanding a warning message from a controller. These observations indicate that, although training and preparation are clearly beneficial in increasing shared repertoires, challenges persist in everyday radio communication, through which pilots and controllers learn in practice. As this experiential learning accumulates, individuals become increasingly expert members – or old-timers – within their communities of practice (Lave, 2019; Lave & Wenger, 1991). Regarding the development of expertise in air traffic control, one Korean controller with eight years of experience, as reported by Kim and Elder (2015), provides insights into the intricacies of expertise that are difficult to disentangle. She observed these complexities within her immediate local community and stated (p. 140):

> I think those senior controllers who have many years of experience can just realise something unusual in a given situation even before a pilot says something to inform us. They don't even attentively listen to the radio, but it's true that they just know it. I think it's possible because they've been in the same or similar situations before. They grasp the whole thing happening by catching just one word and give us the solution. It's amazing that they know why the pilot requests a certain thing, what the pilot needs, and what measures need to be taken. I think that's why we can't undervalue the number of years of experience in this field.

Competence, Wenger (1998) notes, is not something claimed by individuals but is experienced and demonstrated by members through their own engagement in practice. Senior members in communities of practice, he continues to argue, do not merely serve as sources of information; by embodying the history of the practice, they stand as examples of what is achievable, expected, and desirable. These complexities of competence and expertise are confirmed by Ehrenreich's (2009) study of a business community of practice. Confusing messages from a Chinese manager did not cause any misunderstanding for a German manager, as their established relationship over a long-term trajectory enabled accurate inference and mutual understanding. Additionally, while the Chinese participant's accent was unintelligible to the researcher – a non-member of the community – understanding extended beyond linguistic competence, as evidenced by the German participant's perfect comprehension of the Chinese manager, despite being unable to transcribe the messages verbatim. This illustrates how shared histories of mutual engagement serve as resources for the ability to negotiate meaning (Wenger, 1998), even in the absence of explicit verbal negotiation.

Viewing learning and practice through the lens of the community of practice framework, if both English L1 and L2+ pilots and controllers were recognised as members of the international aviation community of practice and learn through their participation in practice, it is unlikely that ICAO's narrow and biased policy – which treats L2+ pilots and controllers as isolated deficiencies rather than as members of the community – would have developed. In this regard, the widely held dichotomy between 'native' and 'non-native' speakers within aviation communities of practice is not only detrimental to the international community but also inherently perpetuates a deceptive understanding of competency, thereby misleading all members. Moreover, it is a significant loss that the L2+ aviation communities are losing many of their experienced members, who are most likely affected by the ICAO English proficiency requirements (see Kim & Elder, 2015); as a result, community members are deprived of irreplaceable opportunities to learn from them.

While exploring the consequences of ICAO's policy and associated tests is a separate area of inquiry (see Kim, forthcoming), it is evident that practice in international radiotelephony communication should be re-situated within its community context, rather than treated as an isolated component assessable independently of its situated context. This point is further elaborated in the next section.

5.3 Research Question 3: Implications for ICAO's English Proficiency Requirements

The third research question addresses *what are the implications of domain specialists' values for ICAO's English proficiency requirements?* The findings of this study, along with previous research, are discussed in relation to ICAO English proficiency requirements described in Section 3.

The inadequacy of ICAO's traditional, linguistically focussed proficiency requirements was discussed in Section 3. However, the question remains as to how the valued aspects identified by domain specialists can be incorporated into assessment or (community-level) evaluation, especially considering that this does not necessarily have to take the form of formal assessment, particularly when the constitutive features of communities of practice are taken into account. In fact, ICAO's English proficiency requirements exemplify a test-driven policy focussed on an efficient and cost-effective means of demonstrating evidence of action (Shohamy, 2001) on safety, rather than addressing genuine safety concerns. This is evidenced by the rating scale's lack of connection to radiotelephony communication in real-life contexts (Fulcher, 2015; Kim,

2024; McNamara, 2010) and by the lack of effort towards standardisation (Section 5.1.4).

First, the exemption of English L1 pilots and controllers is not warranted, not only because of their well-recognised noncompliance with radiotelephony conventions but also because they are members of the international aviation community of practice. They are required to take responsibility for safe and efficient communication and to contribute their fair share of effort, including for their own benefit. Second, the notion of a fixed shelf life (i.e., the recurrent testing policy) for competence is not justified. All international members become more competent every day as they engage in practice over the radio. Their skills for accommodation and managing various accents also improve continuously as they encounter and are exposed to pilots or controllers with varying levels of awareness and experience. Given the high stakes involved – many lives are at risk – vigorous training and awareness-raising are essential at both local and international levels.

I suggest local community-level evaluation for three reasons. First, individual assessment – whether a person achieves or fails to achieve a certain level on a test – places the important issue of how members can communicate safely and efficiently, and what efforts they should make, solely at the individual level. However, as discussed in the previous section, these skills are more meaningfully learned and established within communities of practice. Second, when this issue is addressed at the local community level, the community itself is better positioned to identify its gaps and determine which skills need to be emphasised and developed, whether that involves the use of sufficiently *plain* enough plain English and employing slow speech in abnormal situations or learning the specific (alternative) vocabulary required for such contexts by all international members. Third, when community-level evaluation is conducted, it is more likely to become embedded in the community's culture and have a tangible impact in real-life situations. Experienced members can take the initiative in the evaluation process, assuming responsibility for improving interactions. In this way, the international community can focus on their contributions to improvement rather than assigning blame to other communities.

Regarding assessment in ELF communication contexts more broadly, substantial discussions have highlighted the unsuitability of existing proficiency-focussed English assessment and emphasised the need for the construct to capture and reflect accommodation skills, such as how communication is achieved collaboratively and the capacity to negotiate variable forms (Canagarajah, 2007; Jenkins & Leung, 2014, 2017; McNamara, 2023). However, little progress has been made in the actual development of such assessment, leaving significant work to be done in language testing.

McNamara's (2023) suggestion to adopt a *strong* performance assessment for ELF communication is noteworthy. A strong approach focusses on task performance in real-world contexts based on real-world criteria – such as those valued by domain specialists in this study – which, McNamara argues, is appropriate for assessment in professional purposes, whereas a *weak* approach emphasises language-related aspects, as is common in many existing language tests (McNamara, 1996). Regarding rating scales, Jenkins and Leung's (2017) suggestion to use a binary approach based on communication outcome, such as successful or unsuccessful, well suits the contexts of ELF communication. For example, as one pilot informant points out, the first controller in the episode examined in this study, although his lack of comprehension was negatively evaluated by some informants, was experienced enough to recognise the situation, instruct the following aircraft to execute a go-around, and hand over to the second controller by providing a new, separate frequency to the pilot. While the first controller's comprehension can be discretely evaluated as unsuccessful, his handling of the situation and the handover can, overall, be evaluated positively, as he acted within his own repertoire and did not cause an incident.

Dealing with a variety of English-speaking accents is a linguistic challenge that all pilots and controllers, both English L1 and L2+, unanimously acknowledge; importantly, it is a skill that improves with exposure and experience. In terms of reflecting this reality and incorporating various English accents in assessments, some scholars argue that including a range of accents may disadvantage individuals with little or no prior exposure to certain varieties (e.g., Talyor & Geranpayeh, 2011). This argument illustrates McNamara's (2012) assertion that test constructs represent arenas where competing values are contested. That is, the 'assumed privileges' (p. 201) of the educated 'native speaker' of 'standard English' – often described at the highest levels in rating scales and positioned as the target of achievement for 'non-native speakers' – are challenged when the perspective of ELF is adopted. Thus, while the ultimate goal in language testing is to reflect the real-life performance as closely as possible, incorporating this aspect of reality in ELF contexts is often treated as an exception due to the values at stake. In ELF communication, interlocutors cannot be chosen, and individuals interact with speakers who have varying degrees of experience, domain expertise, or competence. Consequently, managing unfamiliar accents is a challenge that everyone encounters. Moreover, extended exposure to and the ability to comprehend a variety of accents are qualities characteristic of experts in ELF communication.

Lastly, what, then, could be the threshold English proficiency required to enter communities of practice? When a strong approach is adopted, I argue that this question loses much of its significance. While exploring the repertoires that contribute to successful or unsuccessful performance in assessment would be valuable – particularly as this area remains largely understudied – applied linguistics often places undue emphasis on language in isolation, despite language being only one of many factors influencing communication and performance in real-life settings. Membership in communities of practice inherently provides learning opportunities for all participants (Lave, 2019; Lave & Wenger, 1991), who are on a continuous path towards expertise within that community. Therefore, a more holistic understanding of performance (and language use within it) in lingua franca professional contexts is required.

5.4 Concluding Remarks

I attempted to characterise aviation ELF within the framework of communities of practice, focussing on shared and unshared repertoires among members in international radiotelephony communication and emphasising accommodation to bridge gaps. This was achieved by examining naturally occurring discourse and drawing on insights from domain specialists, as well as ICAO English proficiency requirements, in light of what domain experts say and what the framework offers. The non-face-to-face, voice-only radiotelephony communication between pilots and controllers shapes many characteristics of this interaction, while participants' multiple memberships at both local and international levels create a unique communicative context in which diverse values and perceptions are at play. The profound gap between the conceptualised construct represented in the ICAO rating scale and the aspects valued by language users in the target language use situation prevents ICAO from achieving its intended impact – namely, that aviation safety would improve if all speakers had good English proficiency. As in one of the ELF professional contexts, understanding performance cannot be reduced to mere 'English proficiency'. Placing the responsibility for successful communication solely on individuals is an irresponsible policy, as there is much more that needs to be done – and can be done – by ICAO to ensure greater safety and efficiency. Meaningful efforts from responsible international bodies, associated local authorities, and pilot and controller communities are needed through dialogue, collaboration, and genuine engagement. Such efforts are essential to bring about the changes required in real-world settings.

References

Adank, P., Evans, B. G., Stuart-Smith, J., & Scott, S. K. (2009). Comprehension of familiar and unfamiliar native accents under adverse listening conditions. *Journal of Experimental Psychology: Human Perception and Performance*, *35*(2), 520–529. https://doi.org/10.1037/a0013552.

Aeronautica Civil of the Republic of Colombia. (1996). *Aircraft accident report: Controlled flight into terrain, American Airlines Flight 965, Boeing 757–223, N651AA, near Cali, Colombia, December 20, 1995*. D. C. Santafe de Bogota, Colombia.

Alderson, J. C. (2009). Air safety, language assessment policy, and policy implementation: The case of aviation English. *Annual Review of Applied Linguistics*, *29*, 168–187. https://doi.org/10.1017/S0267190509090138.

Alderson, J. C. (2010). A survey of aviation English tests. *Language Testing*, *27*(1), 51–72. https://doi.org/10.1177/0265532209347196.

Alderson, J. C. (2011). The politics of aviation English testing. *Language Assessment Quarterly*, *8*, 386–403. https://doi.org/10.1080/15434 303.2011.622017.

Angell, I. O., & Straub, B. (1999). Rain-dancing with pseudo-science. *Cognition, Technology & Work*, *1*, 179–196. https://doi.org/10.1007/s101110050016.

Aviation Policy Division. (2009). *Open hearing on improvement of aviation English proficiency test*. Ministry of Land, Transport, and Maritime Affairs, Korea.

Aviation Safety Network. (n.d.). *Accident description for Kazakhstan Airlines flight 1907*. http://aviation-safety.net/database/record.php?id=19961112-1.

Bent, T., & Bradlow, A. R. (2003). The interlanguage speech intelligibility benefit. *Journal of the Acoustical Society of America*, *114*(3), 1600–1610. https://doi.org/10.1121/1.1603234.

Besnard, D., Greathead, D., & Baxter, G. (2003). When mental models go wrong: Co-occurrences in dynamic, critical systems. *International Journal of Human-Computer Studies*, *60*, 117–128. https://doi.org/10.1016/j.ijhcs.2003.09.001.

Birlik, S., & Kaur, J. (2020). BELF expert users: Making understanding visible in internal BELF meetings through the use of nonverbal communication stretegies. *English for Specific Purposes*, *58*, 1–14. https://doi.org/10.1016/j.esp.2019.10.002.

Bourhis, R. Y., & Giles, H. (1977). The language of intergroup distinctiveness. In H. Giles (Ed.), *Language, ethnicity and intergroup relations* (pp. 119–135). Academic Press.

References

Braun, V., & Clarke, V. (2006). Using thematic analysis in psychology. *Qualitative Research in Psychology*, *3*(2), 77–101. https://doi.org/10.1191/1478088706qp063oa.

Burki-Cohen, J. (1995). *Analysis of tower (ground) controller-pilot voice communication*. U.S. Department of Transportation.

Campbell-Laird, K. (2004, September–October). Aviation English: A review of the language of international civil aviation. International Professional Communication Conference.

Canagarajah, S. (2007). Lingua franca English, multilingual communities, and language acquisition. *The Modern Language Journal*, *91*(1), 923–939. https://doi.org/10.1111/j.1540-4781.2007.00678.x.

Cardosi, K. M. (1993). *An analysis of en route controller-pilot voice communication*. U.S. Department of Transportation.

Chakrani, B. (2015). Arabic interdialectal encounters: Investigating the influence of attitudes on language accommodation. *Language & Communication*, *41*, 17–27. https://doi.org/10.1016/j.langcom.2014.10.006.

Cilliers, P. (2005). Complexity, deconstruction and relativism. *Theory, Culture & Society*, *22*(5), 255–267. https://doi.org/10.1177/0263276405058052.

Cogo, A. (2009). Accommodating difference in ELF conversations: A study of pragmatic strategies. In A. Mauranen & E. Ranta (Eds.), *English as a lingua franca: Studies and findings* (pp. 254–273). Cambridge Scholars Publishing.

Cooper, E. (1989). Apprenticeship as field method: Lessons from Hong Kong. In M. W. Coy (Ed.), *Apprenticeship: From theory to method and back again* (pp. 137–148). State University of New York Press.

Coy, M. W. (1989). From theory. In M. W. Coy (Ed.), *Apprenticeship: From theory to method and back again* (pp. 1–11). State University of New York Press.

Crystal, D. (2003). *English as a global language* (2nd ed.). Cambridge University Press. https://doi.org/10.1017/CBO9780511486999.

Cushing, S. (1994). *Fatal words*. The University of Chicago Press.

Cushing, S. (1995, July). Pilot-air traffic control communications: It's not (only) what you say, it's how you say it. *Flight Safety Digest*.

De Andrade, N. (2023). The performance of Brazilian air traffic controllers in radiotelephony communication in English: The controllers' perspective. *Applied Linguistics Papers*, *27*(1), 79–90. https://doi.org/10.32612/uw.25449354.2023.1.pp.79-90.

Dekker, S. (2013). *Second victim: Error, guilt, trauma, and resilience*. CRC Press. https://doi.org/10.1201/b14797.

Dekker, S. W. A. (2001). The disembodiment of data in the analysis of human factors accidents. *Human Factors and Aerospace Safety*, *1*(1), 39–57.

Dekker, S. W. A. (2003). Illusions of explanation: A critical essay on error classification. *The International Journal of Aviation Psychology*, *13*(2), 95–106. https://doi.org/10.1207/S15327108IJAP1302_01.

Dekker, S., Cilliers, P., & Hofmeyr, J.-H. (2011). The complexity of failure: Implications of complexity theory for safety investigations. *Safety Science*, *49*(6), 939–945. https://doi.org/10.1016/j.ssci.2011.01.008.

Douglas, D. (2000). *Assessing language for specific purposes*. Cambridge University Press. https://doi.org/10.1017/CBO9780511732911.

Douglas, D. (2023). Specificity, authenticity, and inseparability: Assessing integrated oral skills for pilots and air traffic controllers. *Applied Linguistics Papers*, *27*(1), 4–13. https://doi.org/10.32612/uw.25449354.2023.1.pp.4-13.

Dragojevic, M., Gasiorek, J., & Giles, H. (2016). Accommodative strategies as core of the theory. In H. Giles (Ed.), *Communication accommodation theory: Negotiating personal relationships and social identities across contexts* (pp. 36–59). Cambridge University Press. https://doi.org/10.1017/CBO9781316226537.003.

Drayton, J., & Coxhead, A. (2023). The development, evaluation and application of an aviation radiotelephony specialised technical vocabulary list. *English for Specific Purposes*, *69*, 51–66. https://doi.org/10.1016/j.esp.2022.10.001.

Eckert, P., & Wenger, E. (2005). Communities of practice in sociolinguistics. *Journal of Sociolinguistics*, *9*(4), 582–589. https://doi.org/10.1111/j.1360-6441.2005.00307.x.

Ehrenreich, S. (2009). English as a lingua franca in multinational corporations: Exploring business communities of practice. In A. Mauranen & E. Ranta (Eds.), *English as a lingua franca: Studies and findings* (pp. 126–151). Cambridge Scholars Publishing.

Ehrenreich, S. (2010). English as a business lingua franca in a German ultinational corporation: Meeting the challenge. *Journal of Business Communication*, *47*(4), 408–431. https://doi.org/10.1177/0021943610377303.

Ehrenreich, S. (2017). Communities of practice and English as a lingua franca. In J. Jenkins, W. Baker, & M. Dewey (Eds.), *The Routledge handbook of English as a lingua franca* (pp. 37–50). Routledge.

Elder, C., & McNamara, T. (2016). The hunt for "indigenous criteria" in assessing communication in the physiotherapy workplace. *Language Testing*, *33*(2), 153–174. https://doi.org/10.1177/0265532215607398.

Elder, C., McNamara, T., Kim, H., Pill, J., & Sato, T. (2017). Interrogating the construct of communicative competence in language assessment contexts:

What the non-language specialist can tell us. *Language & Communication*, *57*, 14–21. https://doi.org/10.1016/j.langcom.2016.12.005.

Elder, C., Phill, J., Woodword-Kron, R., McNamara, T., Manias, E., Webb, G., & McColl, G. (2012). Health professionals' views of communication: Implications for assessing performance on a health-specific English language test. *TESOL Quarterly*, *46*(2), 409–419. https://doi.org/10.1002/tesq.26.

Endsley, M. R., & Strauch, B. (1997). Automation and situation awareness: The accident at Cali, Colombia. *Proceedings of the 9th International Symposium on Aviation Psychology*.

Estival, D., Farris, C., & Molesworth, B. (2016). Aviation English: A linguistic description. *Aviation English: A lingua franca for pilots and air traffic controllers* (pp. 22–53). Routledge.

Estival, D. (2025). *Native English speakers and aviation communication*. Routledge. https://doi.org/10.4324/9781003371854.

Friginal, E., Mathews, E., & Roberts, J. (2019). *English in global aviation: Context, research, and pedagogy*. Bloomsbury. https://doi.org/10.5040/9781350059344.

Fulcher, G. (2015). *Re-examining language testing: A philosophical and social inquiry*. Routledge.

Gaete, C. (2022). *Accommodation in English as a lingua franca: A sociopsychological and sociolinguistic study* [Unpublished doctoral dissertation, University of Southhampton].

Galloway, N., & Rose, H. (2015). *Introducing global Englishes* (1st ed.). Routledge. https://doi.org/10.4324/9781315734347.

Gasiorek, J. (2016). Theoretical perspectives on interpersonal adjustments in language and communication. In H. Giles (Ed.), *Communication accommodation theory: Negotiating personal relationships and social identities across contexts* (pp. 13–35). Cambridge University Press. https://doi.org/10.1017/CBO9781316226537.002.

Gibbon, D. (2005). Navigating pronunciation in search of the golden fleece. In K. Dziubalska-Kołaczyk & J. Przedlacka (Eds.), *Pronunciation models: A changing scene* (pp. 439–465). Peter Lang.

Giles, H. (2016). The social origins of CAT. In H. Giles (Ed.), *Communication accommodation theory: Neogotiating personal relationships and social identities across contexts* (pp. 1–12). Cambridge University Press. https://doi.org/10.1017/CBO9781316226537.001.

Giles, H., Coupland, N., & Coupland, J. (1991). Accommodation theory: Communication, context, and consequence. In H. Giles, J. Coupland, & N. Coupland (Eds.), *Context of accommodation: Developments in applied sociolinguistics* (pp. 1–68). Cambridge University Press.

Government of India Civil Aviation Department. (1999). Operations circular No. 3 of 1999. In *Reference No: AV.22029/23/99-FID*. India.

Hawkins, F. H., & Orlady, H. W. (2017). *Human factors in flight* (2nd ed.). Routlege. https://doi.org/10.4324/9781351218580.

Helmreich, R. L. (1994). Anatomy of a system accident: The crash of Avianca Flight 052. *The International Journal of Aviation Psychology*, 4(3), 265–284.

Holliday, A. (2009). English as a lingua franca, "non-native speakers" and cosmopolitan realities. In F. Sharifian (Ed.), *English as an international language: Perspectives and pedagogical issues* (pp. 21–33). Multilingual Matters. https://doi.org/10.21832/9781847691231-005.

Holliday, A. (2018). Native-speakerism. In J. I. Liontas (Ed.), *The TESOL encyclopedia of English language teaching* (pp.1–7). Wiley Blackwell. https://doi.org/10.1002/9781118784235.eelt0027.

House, J. (2003). English as a lingua franca: A threat to multilingualism? *Journal of Sociolinguistics*, 7(4), 556–578. https://doi.org/10.1111/j.1467-9841.2003.00242.x.

Howard, J. W. (2008). "Tower, am I cleared to land?": Problematic communication in aviation discourse. *Human Communication Research*, 34(3), 370–391. https://doi.org/10.1111/j.1468-2958.2008.00325.x.

Hutchins, E., & Klausen, T. (1996). Distributed cognition in an airline cockpit. In Y. Engeström & D. Middleton (Eds.), *Cognition and communication at work* (pp. 15–34). Cambridge University Press.

Hymes, D. (1986). Models of the interaction of language and social life. In J. J. Gumperz & D. Hymes (Eds.), *Directions in sociolinguistics: The ethnography of communication* (pp. 35–71). Basil Blackwell. https://doi.org/10.1111/j.1540-4560.1967.tb00572.x.

ICAO. (1944). *Convention on international civil aviation*. International Civil Aviation Organisation.

ICAO. (1978). *Final report and comment of the Netherlands Aviation Safety Board* (ICAO Circular 153-AN/56). International Civil Aviation Organisation

ICAO. (1996). *Aeronautical telecommunications* (5th ed., Vol. 1 Radio navigation aids). International Civil Aviation Organisation.

ICAO. (2001). *Development of standard (PRICESG second meeting)*. International Civil Aviation Organisation.

ICAO. (2004). *Manual on the implementation of ICAO language proficiency requirements* (1st ed.). International Civil Aviation Organisation.

ICAO. (2007). *Manual of radiotelephony* (4th ed.). International Civil Aviation Organisation.

ICAO. (2010). *Manual on the implementation of ICAO language proficiency requirements* (2nd ed.). International Civil Aviation Organisation.

ICAO. (2016). *Aeronautical telecommunications* (7th ed., Vol. 2 Communication proceures including those with PANS status). International Civil Aviation Organisation.

ICAO. (2022). *Personnel licensing* (14th ed.). International Civil Aviation Organisation.

ICAO. (n.d.). *Flight safety section: Personnel licensing FAQs*. Retrieved July 11, 2013 from http://legacy.icao.int/icao/en/trivia/peltrgFAQ.htm.

Jacoby, S., & McNamara, T. (1999). Locating competence. *English for Specific Purposes, 18*(3), 213–241. https://doi.org/10.1016/S0889-4906(97)00053-7.

Jenkins, J. (2000). *The phonology of English as an international language.* Oxford University Press.

Jenkins, J. (2007). *English as a lingua franca: Attitude and identity.* Oxford University Press.

Jenkins, J. (2022). Accommodation in ELF: Where from? where now? where next? In I. Walkinshow (Ed.), *Pragmatics in English as a lingua franca* (pp. 17–34). De Gruyter. https://doi.org/10.1515/9781501512520-002.

Jenkins, J., & Leung, C. (2014). English as a lingua franca. In A. J. Kunnan (Ed.), *The companion ot language assessment* (1st ed., pp. 1605–1616). John Wiley & Sons. https://doi.org/10.1002/9781118411360.wbcla047.

Jenkins, J., & Leung, C. (2017). Assessing English as a lingua franca. In E. Shohamy, I. G. Or, & S. May (Eds.), *Language testing and assessment* (3rd ed., pp. 103–117). Springer. https://doi.org/10.1007/978-3-319-02261-1_7.

Jones, R. K. (2003). Miscommunication between pilots and air traffic control. *Language Problems and Language Planning, 27*(3), 233–248.

Kaur, J. (2009). *English as a lingua franca: Co-constructing understanding.* VDM Verlag.

Kaur, J., & Birlik, S. (2021). Communicative effectiveness in BELF (English as a Business Lingua Franca) meetings: "Explaining" as a pragmatic strategy. *The Modern Language Journal, 105*(3), 623–638. https://doi.org/10.1111/modl.12717.

Kim, H. (2012). *Exploring the construct of aviation communication: A critique of the ICAO language proficiency policy* [Unpublished doctoral dissertation, University of Melbourne].

Kim, H. (2018). What constitutes professional communication in aviation: Is language proficiency enough for testing purposes? *Language Testing, 35*(3), 403–426. https://doi.org/10.1177/0265532218758127.

Kim, H. (2024). Are we assessing the right abilities for aviation communication? In E. Friginal, M. Prado, & J. Roberts (Eds.), *Global aviation English research* (pp. 117–134). Bloomsbury. https://doi.org/10.5040/9781350411708.ch-7.

Kim, H. (forthcoming). Navigating the consequential aspects of validity through narrative inquiry: When international testing policy lands locally.

Kim, H., & Billington, R. (2018). Pronunciation and comprehension in English as a lingua franca communication: Effect of L1 influence in international aviation communication. *Applied Linguistics*, *39*(2), 135–158. https://doi.org/10.1093/applin/amv075.

Kim, H., & Elder, C. (2009). Understanding aviation English as a lingua franca: Perceptions of Korean aviation personnel. *Australian Review of Applied Linguistics*, *32*(3), 23.21–23.17. https://doi.org/10.2104/aral0923.

Kim, H., & Elder, C. (2015). Interrogating the construct of aviation English: Feedback from test takers in Korea. *Language Testing*, *32*(2), 129–149. https://doi.org/10.1177/0265532214544394.

Kim, H., & Friginal, E. (2025). Washback in language for professional purposes testing: A case of pilot-air traffic controller radiotelephony communication. In D. Allen (Ed.), *Washback research in language assessment: Fundamentals and contexts* (pp. 172–184). Routledge. https://doi.org/10.4324/9781003472681-16.

Kim, H., & Friginal, E. (2026). Revisiting aviation English as a lingua franca: Insights from domain specialists. *Applied Linguistics Review*.

Kim, H., & Penry Williams, C. (2021). *Discovering intercultural communication: From language users to language use*. Palgrave Macmillan. https://doi.org/10.1007/978-3-030-76595-8.

Kim, H., & Zhang, V. X. (forthcoming). Integrating grammatical analysis into English for specific purposes instruction: The case of aviation English.

Knapp, M., Hall, J., & Horgan, T. G. (2014). *Nonverbal communication in human interaction* (8th ed.). Cengage Learning.

Knoch, U. (2014). Using subject specialist to validate an ESP rating scale: The case of the International Civil Aviation Organisation (ICAO) rating scale. *English for Specific Purposes*, *33*, 77–86. https://doi.org/10.1016/j.esp.2013.08.002.

Krause, S. S. (2003). *Aircraft safety: Accident investigations, analyses, and applications*. McGraw-Hill.

Labov, W. (1972). *Sociolinguistic patterns*. University of Pennsylvania Press.

Lave, J. (2019). *Learning and everyday life: Access, participation, and changing practice*. Cambridge University Press. https://doi.org/10.1017/9781108616416.

Lave, J., & Wenger, E. (1991). *Situated learning: Legitimate peripheral participation*. Cambridge University Press.

MacKenzie, D. (2010). *ICAO: A history of the International Civil Aviation Organisation*. University of Toronto Press.

Major, R. C., Fitzmaurice, S. F., Bunta, F., & Balasubramanian, C. (2002). The effects of nonnative accents on listening comprehension: Implications for ESL assessment. *TESOL Quarterly*, *36*(2), 173–190. https://doi.org/10.2307/3588329.

McNamara, T. (1996). *Measuring second language performance*. Longman.

McNamara, T. (2010). The use of language tests in the service of policy: Issues of validity. *Revue Française de Linguistique Appliquée*, *XV*(1), 7–23.

McNamara, T. (2011). Managing learning: Authority and language assessment. *Language Teaching*, *44*(4), 500–515. https://doi.org/10.1017/S0261444811000073.

McNamara, T. (2012). English as a lingua franca: The challenge for language testing. *Journal of English as a Lingua Franca*, *1*(1), 199–202. https://doi.org/10.1515/jelf-2012-0013.

McNamara, T. (2023). A challenge for language testing: The assessment of English as a lingua franca. In K. Murata (Ed.), *ELF and applied linguistics: Reconsidering applied linguistics research from ELF perspectives* (pp. 191–206). Routledge. https://doi.org/10.4324/9781003391463-16.

Mell, J. (1992). *Étude des Communications Verbales entre Pilote et Controleur en Situation Standard et Non-Standard* [doctoral dissertation, Université du Mirail, Toulouse, France (and École Nationale de l'Aviation Civile, Centre d'Études de la Navigation Aérienne)].

Molesworth, B. R. C., Burgess, M., Gunnell, B., Löffler, D., & Venjakob, A. (2014). The effect on recognition memory of noise cancelling headphones in a noisy environment with native and nonnative speakers. *Noise and Health*, *16*(71), 240–247. https://doi.org/10.4103/1463-1741.137062.

Morrow, D., Lee, A., & Rodvold, M. (1993). Analysis of problems in routine controller-pilot communication. *International Journal of Aviation Psychology*, *3*(4), 285–302. https://doi.org/10.1207/s15327108ijap0304_3.

Morrow, D., Rodvold, M., & Lee, A. (1994). Nonroutine transactions in controller-pilot communication. *Discourse Processes*, *17*(2), 235–258. https://doi.org/10.1080/01638539409544868.

Murtaugh, M. (1985). The practice of arithmetic by American grocery shoppers. *Anthropology & Education Quarterly*, *16*(3), 186–192. https://www.jstor.org/stable/3216562.

NTSB. (1991). *Aircraft accident report: Avianca, the airline of Columbia, Boeing 707-321B, HK2016, fuel exhaustion, Cove Neck, New York, January 25, 1990*. National Transportation Safety Board.

NTSB. (n.d.). *Boeing submission to the American Airlines 965 Accident Investigation Board*. National Transportation Safety Board.

Orasanu, J. M. (1994). Shared problem models and flight crew performance. In N. Johnston & N. McDonald (Eds.), *Aviation psychology in practice* (pp. 255–285). Routledge. https://doi.org/10.4324/9781351218825.

Oswald, M. E., & Grosjean, S. (2004). Confirmation bias. In R. F. Pohl (Ed.), *Cognitive illusions: A handbook on fallacies and biases in thinking, judgement and memory* (pp. 79–96). Psychology Press. https://doi.org/10.4324/9780203720615.

Park, J. S.-Y. (2009). *The local construction of a global language: Ideologies of English in South Korea*. Mouton de Gruyter. https://doi.org/10.1515/9783110214079.

Philps, D. (1991). Linguistic security in the syntactic structures of air traffic control English. *English World-Wide*, *12*(1), 103–124. https://doi.org/10.1075/eww.12.1.07phi.

Pill, J. (2016). Drawing on indigenous criteria for more authentic assessment in a specific-purpose language test: Health professionals interacting with patients. *Language Testing*, *33*(2), 175–193. https://doi.org/10.1177/0265532215607400.

Piller, I. (2002). Passing for a native speaker: Identity and success in second language learning. *Journal of Sociolinguistics*, *6*(2), 179–206. https://doi.org/10.1111/1467-9481.00184.

Piller, I., & Bodis, A. (2022). Marking and unmarking the (non)native speaker through English language proficiency requirements for university admission. *Language in Society*, *53*(1), 1–23. https://doi.org/10.1017/S0047404522000689.

Pitzl, M.-L. (2009). "We should not wake up any dogs": Idiom and metaphor in ELF. In A. Mauranen & E. Ranta (Eds.), *English as a lingua franca: Studies and findings* (pp. 298–322). Cambridge Scholars Publishing.

Prinzo, O. V., Hendrix, A. M., & Hendrix, R. (2008). *Pilot English language proficiency and the prevalence of communication problems at five US air route traffic control centers*. Federal Aviation Administration.

Robertson, F. A. (1987). *Airspeak: Radiotelephony communication for pilots*. Prentice Hall.

Roitsch, P. A., Babcock, G. L., & Edmunds, W. W. (1978). *Human factors report on the Tenerife accident*. Air Line Pilots Association.

Sato, T., & McNamara, T. (2019). What counts in second language oral communicaiton ability?: The perspective of linguistic laypersons. *Applied Linguistics*, *40*(6), 894–916. https://doi.org/10.1093/applin/amy032.

Seidlhofer, B. (2009). Accommodation and the idiom principle in English as a lingua franca. *Intercultural Pragmatics*, *6*(2), 195–215. https://doi.org/10.1515/IPRG.2009.011.

Shimizu, T., Makishima, K., Yoshida, M., & Yamagishi, H. (2002). Effect of background noise on perception of English speech for Japanese listeners. *Auris Nasus Larynx*, *29*(2), 121–125. https://doi.org/10.1016/S0385-8146(01)00133-X.

Shohamy, E. (2001). *The power of tests: A critical perspective on the uses of language tests*. Longman.

Simmon, D. A. (1998). Boeing 757 CFIT accident at Cali, Colombia, becomes focus of lessons learned. *Fight Safety Digest*, *17*(5/6), 1–31.

Smith, L. E., & Nelson, C. L. (2020). World Englishes and issues of intelligibility. In C. L. Nelson, Z. G. Proshina, & D. R. Davis (Eds.), *The handbook of world Englishes* (2nd ed., pp. 430–446). Wiley Blackwell. https://doi.org/10.1002/9781119147282.ch24.

Strauch, B. (1997). *Automation and decision making: Lessons from the Cali accident*. Proceedings of the Human Factors and Ergonomics Society 41st Annual Meeting.

Strauss, A., & Corbin, J. (1994). Grounded theory methodology: An overview. In N. K. Denzin & Y. S. Lincoln (Eds.), *Handbook of qualitative research* (pp. 273–285). Sage Publications.

Subsecretaria de Aviacion Civil. (1978). *KLM, B-747, PH-BUF and Pan Am B-747 N736 collision at Tenerife airport Spain on 27 March 1977*. Subsecretaria de Aviacion Civil, Spain.

Tajima, A. (2004). Fatal miscommunication: English in aviation safety. *World Englishes*, *23*(3), 451–470. https://doi.org/10.1111/j.0883-2919.2004.00368.x.

Talyor, L., & Geranpayeh, A. (2011). Assessing listening for academic purposes: Defining and operatationaliazing the test construct. *Journal of English for Academic Purposes*, *10*(2), 89–101. https://doi.org/10.1016/j.jeap.2011.03.002.

Tauroza, S., & Luk, J. (1997). Accent and second language listening comprehension. *RELC Journal*, *28*(1), 54–71. https://doi.org/10.1177/003368829702800104.

Tiewtrakul, T., & Fletcher, S. R. (2010). The challenge of regional accents for aviation English language proficiency standards: A study of difficulties in understanding in air traffic control-pilot communication. *Ergonomics*, *53*(2), 229–239. https://doi.org/10.1080/00140130903470033.

Trippe, J., & Baese-Berk, M. (2019). A prosodic profile of American aviation English. *English for Specific Purposes*, *53*, 30–46. https://doi.org/10.1016/j.esp.2018.08.006.

van Wijngaarden, S. J., Steeneken, H. J. M., & Houtgast, T. (2002). Quantifying the intelligibility of speech in noise for non-native listeners. *Journal of the Acoustical Society of America*, *111*(4), 1906–1916. https://doi.org/10.1121/1.1456928.

Varantola, K. (1989). Natural languages vs. purpose-built languages: The human factors. *Neuphilologische Mitteilungen*, *90*(2), 173–183. https://www.jstor.org/stable/43343925.

Weick, K. E. (1990). The vulnerable system: An analysis of the Tenerife air disaster. *Journal of Management*, *16*(3), 571–593. https://doi.org/10.1177/014920639001600304.

Wenger, E. (1998). *Communities of practice: Learning, meaning, and identity*. Cambridge University Press. https://doi.org/10.1017/CBO9780511803932.

Acknowledgements

I would first like to express my gratitude to the pilots and air traffic controllers who participated in this study and generously shared their expertise and insights, which were instrumental in deepening my understanding of radiotelephony discourse and performance. I am also indebted to Captain Jinwoo Chang for introducing me to the literature on aircraft accidents, which broadened my perspective. I appreciate the Airline Pilots Association, International and The Boeing Company for kindly granting permission to reproduce the figures included in this book, as well as Han Hui Gu for creating the illustrations featured throughout. Finally, I am grateful to the editors, Professors Zhu Hua and Li Wei, and the two reviewers for their valuable feedback, which enabled me to improve my manuscript.

For Cathie and in memory of Tim

Cambridge Elements ⩵

Applied Linguistics

Li Wei
University College London

Li Wei is Chair of Applied Linguistics at the UCL Institute of Education, University College London (UCL), and Fellow of Academy of Social Sciences, UK. His research covers different aspects of bilingualism and multilingualism. He was the founding editor of the following journals: *International Journal of Bilingualism* (Sage), *Applied Linguistics Review* (De Gruyter), *Language, Culture and Society* (Benjamins), *Chinese Language and Discourse* (Benjamins) and *Global Chinese* (De Gruyter), and is currently Editor of the *International Journal of Bilingual Education and Bilingualism* (Taylor and Francis). His books include the *Blackwell Guide to Research Methods in Bilingualism and Multilingualism* (with Melissa Moyer) and *Translanguaging: Language, Bilingualism and Education* (with Ofelia Garcia) which won the British Association of Applied Linguistics Book Prize.

Zhu Hua
University College London

Zhu Hua is Professor of Language Learning and Intercultural Communication at the UCL Institute of Education, University College London (UCL) and is a Fellow of Academy of Social Sciences, UK. Her research is centred around multilingual and intercultural communication. She has also studied child language development and language learning. She is book series co-editor for *Routledge Studies in Language and Intercultural Communication* and *Cambridge Key Topics in Applied Linguistics*, and Forum and Book Reviews Editor of *Applied Linguistics* (Oxford University Press).

About the Series

Mirroring the Cambridge Key Topics in Applied Linguistics, this Elements series focuses on the key topics, concepts and methods in Applied Linguistics today. It revisits core conceptual and methodological issues in different subareas of Applied Linguistics. It also explores new emerging themes and topics. All topics are examined in connection with real-world issues and the broader political, economic and ideological contexts.

Cambridge Elements

Applied Linguistics

Elements in the Series

Kongish: Translanguaging and the Commodification of an Urban Dialect
Tong King Lee

Metalinguistic Awareness in Second Language Reading Development
Sihui Echo Ke, Dongbo Zhang and Keiko Koda

Crisis Leadership: Boris Johnson and Political Persuasion during the Covid Pandemic
Philip Seargeant

Writing Banal Inequalities: How to Fabricate Stories Which Disrupt
Edited by Hannah Cowan and Alfonso Del Percio

New Frontiers in Language and Technology
Christopher Joseph Jenks

Multimodality and Translanguaging in Video Interactions
Maria Grazia Sindoni

A Semiotics of Muslimness in China
Ibrar Bhatt

Narrative and Religion in the Superdiverse City
Stephen Pihlaja

Trans-studies on Writing for English as an Additional Language
Yachao Sun and Ge Lan

Investigating Plagiarism in Second Language Writing
Jun Lei and Guangwei Hu

Discourse, Materiality and Agency within Everyday Social Interactions
Dariush Izadi

Aviation English as a Global Lingua Franca
Hyejeong Kim

A full series listing is available at www.cambridge.org/EIAL

For EU product safety concerns, contact us at Calle de José Abascal, 56–1°, 28003 Madrid, Spain or eugpsr@cambridge.org.

www.ingramcontent.com/pod-product-compliance
Lightning Source LLC
LaVergne TN
LVHW011850060526
838200LV00054B/4273